Human Rights Counterpublics in Perú

DISSIDENT FEMINISMS

Elora Halim Chowdhury, Editor

For a list of books in the series, please see our website at www.press.uillinois.edu.

Human Rights Counterpublics in Perú

Contesting Tiers of Citizenship

SYLVANNA M. FALCÓN

UNIVERSITY OF
ILLINOIS PRESS
Urbana, Chicago, and Springfield

Material from chapters 1 and 2 were first published in the *International Journal of Transitional Justice* (2018): 26–44, https://doi.org/10.1093/ijtj/ijx028, and is reprinted with permission from Oxford University Press.

© 2024 by the Board of Trustees
of the University of Illinois
All rights reserved
1 2 3 4 5 C P 5 4 3 2 1
∞ This book is printed on acid-free paper.

Cataloging-in-Publication Data available from the Library of Congress
ISBN 978-0-252-04603-2 (cloth : alk.)
ISBN 978-0-252-08813-1 (paper : alk.)
ISBN 978-0-252-04721-3 (ebook)

*To the activists, artists, and feminist visionaries
of Perú who have captured
my heart and who inspire me from afar.*

*A las activistas, artistas y visionarias feministas
de Perú que han cautivado
mi corazón y que me inspiran desde la distancia.*

Contents

Preface: Remembering and Reimagining Perú
from the Diaspora   ix

Acknowledgments   xiii

Introduction: Decolonial Feminism, Transitional Justice,
and Counterpublics Activating Human Rights Memory   1

1 Backlash to Building Human Rights Memory   23

2 Memory Recovery through Art and Education   51

3 *No Somos Invisibles*: Domestic Workers
and La Casa de Panchita   71

4 Ghosts, Hauntings, and Unsettling
the Tiers of Citizenship   94

Epilogue   108

Notes   119

Bibliography   127

Index   135

Preface

Remembering and Reimagining Perú from the Diaspora

On May 14, 1966, two people from Perú arrived in the United States with very little money and minimal to no English language skills. They landed in Miami, Florida, eventually making their way to a Greyhound bus to travel to Wichita, Kansas, their final destination. Those two people are my parents. When they arrived in the United States, they were full of dreams, full of fear, and full of uncertainty. Imagining themselves to be temporary visitors here, they planned to return to Perú at some point, but that return never happened.

My dad completed medical school in Perú in an under-resourced public university called San Marcos University. He would often tell my brothers and me about how he had to race to the university library after class to borrow books because he couldn't afford them. The way my dad tells the story, it was an Olympics-style race to the library every single day and he won either the gold or the silver medal each time.

Newly married to my mom, my dad took a medical exam to secure entry into the United States. He and a handful of his male friends passed it and then, with their wives, they were sent to work and further their studies in rural parts of this country. What a deeply isolating experience that must have been for them, to be away from all that was familiar.

I had always been told as a child that this opportunity to migrate presented itself because there was a shortage of doctors in the United States. The doctor shortage, it bears noting, was due to the Vietnam War. A point I made to my mom in a recent conversation is that perhaps their migration to the United States would never have happened had it not been for that catastrophic war. She paused and said, "I suppose that's true, yes."

By the end of 1966, with my parents living here for just a few months, Dr. Martin Luther King Jr. started to publicly denounce the Vietnam War and U.S. imperialism, giving his famous "Beyond Vietnam" speech at Riverside Church the following year on April 4, 1967. Assassinated one year to the day after giving that seminal anti-war speech, Dr. King died on April 4, 1968. My parents had not been in this country for even two years.[1]

Lima, Perú, 1970s–1984

In my youth, every summer for several years, my family would pack up and travel to Lima, Perú. These trips felt mandatory and became part of my summer routine as a child. Our destination was always Lima. We went to see family, and occasionally took trips elsewhere in the country or to other parts of South America. Adjusting to life in Perú was not easy for this kid born in the United States, and at the time I rarely thought about the privileges I took for granted, including the ability to take warm showers and having access to clean drinking water without having to boil it first. Yet there was something freeing about being in a large Peruvian city that I did not experience in the United States, even though my family lived in safe cities and suburbs. In Lima, kids were out and about in the neighborhood, and my mom, normally fearful of us being out of her sight when we were in the United States, seemed quite comfortable with letting me hang out with my older cousins in Perú without adult supervision.

But then the trips suddenly stopped. I remember my grandmother becoming gravely ill in 1984 and my mom returning to Lima with my younger brother, who was about three years old at the time, and thinking, at least for a fleeting moment, about the trip being dangerous for them based on things I had overheard in my parents' conversations. Back then I did not fully understand what it meant to knowingly travel into a situation that might be dangerous. A cholera outbreak occurred shortly after my mom and brother had arrived in Lima, and they returned sooner than anticipated. My grandmother passed away the following week.

By the 1980s we were no longer taking our annual trips to Lima. In fact, I vividly remember one of my last visits there as a kid, when I was about eight or nine years old, and we were having dinner by candlelight at the home of my parents' longtime friends. When I quietly asked why no lights were working, my dad's friend said, "The terrorists bombed the electric company." What in the world were terrorists? And why would they bomb the electric company? I nodded my head even though I had no idea why anyone would want to shut down the city's electricity. Now I know that the terrorist group that had bombed the electric company that night was Sendero Luminoso, the Shining Path.

As I reflect on this vivid childhood memory of having dinner by candlelight, I am surprised that we went to Lima at that time. Was it perhaps in part because the terrorism ravaging parts of the country in the mountains of the Andes felt largely distant from Lima, as only occasional, though often brutal, incidents occurred in this capital city? Is it because being at such a geographical distance, my parents, who now lived in the United States, did not fully comprehend the extent of the terrorism? I still do not know the answers to these questions—a quandary that perhaps speaks to perpetual familial silence about the internal conflict—but I do know that when my family returned in the mid-1990s after an extended period of absence, Lima had changed aesthetically. This was the era of President Alberto Fujimori. And this is where my book begins.

Acknowledgments

The last several years of my life have been about this book, wondering if I had it in me to write another one. As I started to plug away at the research, the data analysis, and the writing, I was constantly reflecting on my life, always wondering what my life would have been like if my parents had not migrated to the United States from Perú. Every time I am in Perú, I ponder where I would have lived, what my career would have been, what challenges I would have faced there in contrast to the life challenges I have had in the United States. The financial security my parents achieved in the United States enabled them to help their families "back home" in Lima, provide for their children (myself and two brothers), and now spoil their grandchildren. This good fortune is perhaps why I see my mom, now in her 80s, still processing how a country could give our family so much opportunity while crushing those same opportunities for other immigrants and US people of color. Of course, that is the point, I tell her—for some to excel, for others to live in perpetual struggle and precarity, for us to see each other in a divisive manner, to ensure that we do not see our freedoms as intertwined, as interconnected, to see our immigrant family's hard work as somehow deserving of stability in comparison to those who also work hard but never are able to attain similar security or stability.

Migration is a complex and emotional experience, and my parents did not have the treacherous experience of so many migrants of being displaced by wars or the climate or something else beyond their control. In my parents' migration story to the United States, which I referenced in the Preface, we have newly arrived immigrants trying to make sense of a foreign land that had a racial history totally unfamiliar to them while at the same time trying to survive. Their early years in the United States happened at a time of tremendous domestic and global unrest, which is also how it feels in the present moment with its global pandemics, natural disasters, and ongoing wars. The birth of this book has only been possible thanks to their brave decision to migrate to this strange and complicated country in 1966. Thanks, Mom and Dad.

I also want to acknowledge the support of other family, friends, and colleagues as well as the various sources of funding that enabled this research to be completed. Thank you to my parents-in-law, Ron and Louise Lehman, for raising such a wonderful son, my lovely husband Matthew. Ron passed away in August 2023 and I miss him and our conversations so very much. Thank you, dearest Matt, for everything, and for working so hard alongside me to build a life together that my immigrant parents and your immigrant grandparents probably could never have imagined possible. Special thanks to our daughter Aracely, who was with me on every single research trip to Lima. She sat through many interviews, field observations, and other conversations as I conducted this research. I even caught her reading an early draft of one of the book chapters where she proudly found a typo and referred to herself then as my editor!

During the writing of this book, I realized that I really love to write in beautiful places. Thus, I want to acknowledge and express my deepest sense of gratitude to the land and the natural beauty that surrounds me in California, especially the areas of Bodega Bay, Half Moon Bay, Mill Valley, Carmel, and Santa Cruz. The pandemic created challenges to my writing retreat getaways, so I embraced the beautiful area I am so lucky to live in with writing retreats in nearby lovely mountain destinations.

I want to acknowledge and express gratitude to so many wonderful colleagues and friends who have supported me in different ways as I completed this book. Much appreciation to my colleagues at UC Santa Cruz, including in my amazing department of Latin American and Latino Studies and beyond—specifically Noriko Ako, Gabriela Arredondo, Kent Eaton, Jennifer Gonzalez, Shelly Grabe, Jody Greene, Kirsten Silva Gruesz, Rebecca Hernandez, Rebecca Hurdis, Kim Lau, Dean Mathiowetz, Teresa Mora, Christina Navarro, Dard Neuman, Ursula Oberg, Patricia Pinho, Justin Perez, Irena Polić, Catherine Ramírez, Shelley Stamp, Jessica Taft, Jennifer Taylor, Veronica Terriquez, and Alice Yang. Thanks also to my awesome friends, especially Kimberly Henderson, Sekou Franklin, Sharmila Lodhia, Molly Talcott, Dana Collins, Hillary Haldane, Ed Peistrup, Lori Sullivan, Michelle Labrador, Molly Milano, Leisy Abrego, Carlos Colorado, Casey Coonerty Protti, and Shannon Gleeson.

Writing an academic book is never a solo endeavor and so my gratitude also goes to Juan Diego Prieto, who provided early research support, my amazing copyeditors Ivo Fravashi and Renee Cote, and the entire staff and team at the University of Illinois Press, especially Acquisitions Editor Dominique J. Moore and Assistant Acquisitions Editor S. Leigh Ann Cowan, as well as the series editor of Dissident Feminisms, Elora Halim Chowdhury. I also want to thank the anonymous external reviewers of the manuscript, whose insightful feedback gave me the guidance needed to improve this final version of the book. Any errors or shortcomings are my own.

Various funding sources at UC Santa Cruz merit recognition for supporting this research and making it possible to complete. Thanks to funding from the Division of Social Sciences, the Dolores Huerta Research Center for the Americas, the Committee on Research, the Merrill College Apprenticeship Program, and the Gary D. Licker Memorial Chair of Cowell College.

Human Rights Counterpublics in Perú

Introduction

Decolonial Feminism, Transitional Justice, and Counterpublics Activating Human Rights Memory (Lima, 2008-2011)

In 2003 I traveled to Lima on my own as a researcher for my dissertation, and then starting in 2008 I returned to begin conducting the research for this book. In 2008 I connected with an organization called La Casa de Panchita. I first read about Panchita in a BBC Mundo article[1] that described the organization's work with domestic workers in Lima—specifically empowering them not only to know their rights but also to be able to advocate for them. Panchita also served as an interface between workers and employers, with the explicit intention of minimizing or eliminating exploitation. This had too often been the experience of domestic workers in Lima, who were completely disempowered and taken advantage of by employers who had no labor regulations to follow, and suffered excessive exploitation and abuse. It remains primarily rural Andean, Amazonian, Indigenous, campesina, and Indian women domestic workers who continue to experience exploitative labor conditions. Though I did not directly ask these women if the Peruvian internal conflict of 1980–2000 had prompted their relocation to Lima, many came from the regional communities that had experienced disproportionate levels of violence during those two decades. The legacy of violence and displacement exacerbated by the internal conflict meant that thousands of people had to build their lives and experiences in a new place.

My time at Panchita revealed the way I, a child of the diaspora, had suppressed memory from afar. In the 2000s my memories of the internal conflict and knowledge about Perú's history of military dictatorship and unrest were largely intellectually known and not viscerally felt. As I spent time at Panchita in the late 2000s and talked with the women who used its services, the aftermath of the internal conflict became difficult to ignore. The fear, distrust, and uncertainty about the future that have become culturally embedded were part of daily life for these women. The displaced Andean and campesina women now living in and around Lima are reminders that the misogyny and racism that contributed to the formation of the Peruvian state have produced what I refer to as "tiers of citizenship" to symbolize the differential value that the state places on human lives.

In 2013 I expanded my research to more directly engage the internal conflict by examining the process of Perú's Truth and Reconciliation Commission, known as the Comisión de la Verdad y Reconciliación (CVR), and by learning about how community activists and artists planned to commemorate the legacy of the internal conflict in 2013, the ten-year anniversary of the CVR's final report. At this time, I connected to artists and activists who were provoking debate about the internal conflict through their work, which challenged a dominant narrative emerging from the political right about former president Fujimori. This narrative asserted that even if Fujimori's administration crossed the line when it came to citizens' rights, he had had no choice, because the insurgency groups needed to be forcibly stopped. These artists sought to convey a more complex memory based on dignity and human rights.

The official end of an internal conflict can be marked by the establishment of a truth commission or by the signing of a peace accord, and is referred to as a period of "transitional justice." When a country has undergone widespread human rights violations, in which its society is left fragmented and disoriented, there can be political will and pressure to reckon with the brutal past in the hope of a brighter future. Perú has engaged in the transitional justice process with mixed results, and this book contends that these dissatisfying outcomes are related to the fraught terrain of memory.

The Peruvian internal conflict differs from others in Latin America. Sendero Luminoso, or the Shining Path, was a communist armed insurgency group in Perú that exhibited extreme and vulgar forms of violence against Indigenous groups as well as activists affiliated with unions or women's groups. Unlike other insurgencies of the 1960s and 1970s in countries such as Argentina and Chile or in the countries of Central America, Sendero Luminoso intentionally targeted civilian groups. In other words, Sendero Luminoso is different than other armed insurgencies, as it has a direct and contributing role in the trauma and sociopolitical violence that haunts the country today. Further, the Peruvian state military and police forces that engaged in counterinsurgency campaigns exacerbated widespread trauma through their own indiscriminate targeting of civilian groups.

Social violence refers to the everyday injustices that pervade daily life, felt especially acutely by those who reside on the margins of society and which intensified during the internal conflict. The haunting of unresolved social violence results in the normalization of perpetual stigmatization and marginalization and was the undercurrent of the two-decades-long internal conflict. The way to change the future course of a country, to grapple with the haunting itself, is through decolonial feminism, which involves engaging with truth-telling, forgiveness, and reconciliation that go far beyond solely legal approaches to justice.

This book seeks to build on decolonial feminist approaches to transitional justice in which the focus of research moves beyond the legal realm as the primary site for recognizing societal approaches and responses in the post-conflict period.[2] More importantly, in drawing from decolonial feminist approaches to transitional justice, I do not endorse the temporal logic that delineates a rigid start and an end date of the internal conflict. For the sake of clarity, though, I reference key dates during the two decades of internal conflict (1980–2000) with an acknowledgment that there are precedents and antecedents, specifically in Chapter 1.

Activating memory alongside decolonial feminism can undo tiers of citizenship. I selected the word "tiers" in relation to citizenship, in part, because its pronunciation is the same as "tears." And a meaningful engagement with decolonial feminism requires a deep connection to emotion, to an understanding that there may be instances in which words cannot convey the pain and that a release of tears is warranted to arrive at new understandings about the possibility of coexistence. The tiers of citizenship embedded in Peruvian society have created a societal hierarchy and divisions that are at the core of failing to recognize lives as interconnected and intertwined.

Decolonial Feminist Perspectives on Transitional Justice and Human Rights Memory

Dating back to the establishment of the United Nations in 1945, numerous countries throughout the world have engaged in some form of transitional justice during a postwar or postconflict period. Transitional justice is about "a range of approaches that societies undertake to reckon with legacies of widespread or systematic human rights abuses as they move from a period of violent conflict or oppression towards peace, democracy, the rule of law, and respect for individual and collective rights."[3] In other words, transitional justice is a time when "healing of the wounds and closure of the conflict [can happen] so the parties can live together."[4] The goals of transitional justice are to decipher largely legal remediation, to render punitive justice to perpetrators through criminal courts, and to analyze what happened during the internal conflict that left the country vulnerable to widespread violence.

The idea of transitions suggests an end goal or end point. But how can a society built on social hierarchies or tiers of citizenship accomplish such an undertaking? How does a society move from transitional or transitioning to transitioned? Like so many countries throughout the world, societal transitions are ongoing and start anew with each generation. The aftermath of a conflict does not organically remove the roots of the causes of the conflict itself.

Perú is a majority Indigenous country and one of the most economically disadvantaged in the Americas region. Its widespread human rights violations occurred while a democratically elected government was in power, and its extreme wealth disparity dates back to the hacienda period. The seeds that grew into the internal conflict in 1980 were planted much earlier, during the formation of the Peruvian nation-state; social violence did not come out of nowhere.[5] Following decades of military rule, Perú had transitioned into a democracy that kept intact sociocultural exclusion, wealth disparities, and a lack of real security and opportunities for mobility. Two decades of an internal conflict resulted in the deaths of nearly seventy thousand people, and thousands disappeared. Unlike internal conflicts in other Latin American countries, such as Guatemala, Argentina, and Chile, the Peruvian internal conflict started with the transition to a democratically elected government after decades of military rule, and also involved the culpability of nonstate actors in committing egregious human rights violations.[6] Any kind of transition would have to confront those truths in order to envision and enact a new norm of justice.

Periods of transition from conflict to postconflict create an opening in which a country and its people can, to some degree, build anew, with newly elected democratic governance, the rewriting of national constitutions, the establishment of new laws and legal precedents, and even criminal trials for human rights violations (consider the Nuremberg trials in the 1950s and, in the case of Perú, the 2007 trial of ex-president Alberto Fujimori). These transitional justice moments can offer hope at a time of extreme pain and trauma. Producing or documenting memories through art, by both state and nonstate social actors, has been one of many generative outcomes of the Peruvian transitional justice period. Art projects that are independent of state-led transitional justice initiatives convey a perspective about the internal conflict and the state's legacy of marginalization that is in tension with the discourse from the dominant public that seeks to absolve the state and urban elites of culpability.

However, the temporal logic of classifying the political internal conflict as being contained within the two decades of the 1980s and 1990s suggests a lack of sociopolitical conflicts, or fewer conflicts, before 1980 and after 2000. If anything, the social realities prior to the official start of the internal conflict on May 17, 1980—when Sendero Luminoso rebels burned the ballot box in Chuschi in the department of Ayacucho—were ripe for a group like Sendero Luminoso to flourish. Today, the underlying causes of the internal armed conflict—racism, social exclusion, patriarchy, and poverty—have led to state-sanctioned violence associated with what can be considered Perú's *new* internal conflict involving the mining industries.[7] And yet this deepening form of extractivist capitalism (exemplified through mining) demonstrates the relative continuity of conflict in a nation-state fundamentally shaped by Spanish settler-colonialism and Indigenous genocide and displacement as well as slavery. And as such, a decolonial feminist lens enables us to most clearly see how a just future might—and must—be built in the twenty-first century.

A decolonial feminist analysis reveals the limitations of the liberalism that is embedded in a capitalist and white supremacist heteropatriarchy the world over. Globally, the threat of authoritarianism in seats of democracy such as the United States and Brazil, to name just two, has at times led to a robust defense of existing institutions and structures. This being the case, many suggest that a way to counter authoritarian regimes is by defending existing government institutions and returning to the "rule of law" (i.e., the status quo). By calling for an emboldened liberalism, the same people who reject authoritarianism do not consider the failures of liberalism that resulted in the election of repressive regimes, even during periods of democracy.

A decolonial feminist analysis challenges both the rise of authoritarianism in democratic societies and the limits of liberalism. A segment of people will always resist authoritarianism, often at great personal cost. Such communities of resistance create and form counterpublics that question sociopolitical hierarchies and advance human rights that are not wedded to liberalism, including the juridical. Culture and art have a critical role to play in these transitional justice efforts and in cultivating human rights memory.

Since 2001, following the resignation of Fujimori in 2000, which is considered to be the official end of the internal conflict, Perú "has used virtually every tool in the transitional justice toolkit" from official apologies to successful prosecutions and convictions of human rights violators.[8] Former president Alberto Fujimori received a twenty-five-year sentence for human rights violations in 2009, but was given a controversial presidential pardon on December 24, 2017, by former president Pedro Pablo Kuczynski (known as PPK) that was widely viewed as a secret deal with Fujimori's politician daughter, Keiko, who was at the forefront of a right-wing movement wanting to oust PPK. Due to the threat of a second impeachment vote, PPK announced his resignation on March 21, 2018. His resignation due to dubious claims of wrongdoing is an indication of the power of the political forces that continue to support Fujimori, most notably including his daughter Keiko.

Transitional justice in Perú remains largely understudied.[9] By focusing on human rights counterpublics, this book extends research on transitional justice beyond an analysis of what the state does and does not do. This research aims to circumvent politics and power at the top and examine what people at the urban local level, specifically in Lima, are doing to facilitate cultural transformations that reflect an approach to human rights that goes beyond establishing legal norms. The communities at the core of my research program are those whom I refer to as belonging to "counterpublics," which are oppositional spaces, movements, and communities challenging the mainstream and the status quo. The status quo in this case represents an entrenched investment in aiming to silence the production of what the late renowned Peruvian cultural anthropologist Carlos Iván Degregori described as an "active memory." For Degregori, who also served on Perú's CVR, a transition from "a kind of passive sympathy to an active memory of the past . . . [is] capable of creating new meanings of the past and political proposals for the future."[10]

By and large, scholars view transitional justice in the realms of the juridical and the political as a genealogy that dates back to the 1940s.[11] My research underscores the effectiveness of the legal and political as important components of transitional justice, but the primary focus is on the sociocultural dimensions of transitional justice that aim to reach the broader Peruvian public. Adopting improved laws is not enough, nor does putting human rights abusers in jail result in a potential turn toward the transformative justice needed for restoration. Criminal trials that end in convictions of human rights perpetrators, while clearly important and necessary, are insufficient because the process of transitional justice is ongoing. Criminal convictions can also be hampered by political corruption, as in the case of Fujimori's controversial pardon at the end of 2017, though the Supreme Court eventually annulled the pardon in October 2018 and he returned to prison.[12] Moreover, just because a certain military general or even former president is now in prison does not mean that affected communities are able to move on. Nor does it mean that their intimate experiences with violence are being somehow validated. These legal and political victories of accountability are not aligned with generations of trauma resulting from wars, social unrest, internal conflicts, and widespread political corruption.

Policies and prosecutions cannot wash away the multigenerational trauma that Peruvians have experienced—trauma that stretches back centuries, predating the establishment of Perú as a nation-state born of colonialism. While the liberalism that underpins political and juridical approaches to transition can indeed promote steadiness, it is a stability grounded in the liberal state's allegiance to a linear narrative of progress. The state's officially sanctioned transitional justice memory defines and confines Peruvians' traumas to those to which the state can offer a solution. However, multigenerational trauma resulting from poverty, racism, misogyny, and colonialism, as well as from the internal conflict, is deeply held within the bodies, spirits, and cultures of everyday Peruvians. And thus, it is to the art, activism, and voices of Peruvians that I turn as I, a child of the diaspora, wonder with urgency, will the future be decolonized? And if so, how? *Human Rights Counterpublics in Perú* takes up these questions by centering on artistic and activist praxes led by counterpublics, as these interventions, I argue, are best equipped to imagine more capacious forms of decolonial healing and transformation than the liberal, transitional state.

The state does not dispute the extent of the terror and violence wrought by Sendero Luminoso (Shining Path) and the Movimiento Revolucionario de Túpac Amaru (Revolutionary Movement of Túpac Amaru [MRTA]), but it does attempt to rationalize, minimize, and justify the "blind repression" egregiously enacted by the military and police. The historian Cynthia Milton argues that this difference results in the creation of narratives that contribute to "human rights memory" and "salvation memory." She writes, "In 'salvation memory,' espoused mainly by the armed forces and neoliberal elites, human rights violations were committed by a few rogue elements in the armed forces, Fujimori's heavy hand and disregard for human rights was the price for breaking the Shining Path, Shining Path as instigator was thus solely responsible for the violence, and 'we' in Lima did not really know the extent of what was going on (and with this lack of knowledge comes a kind of absolution)."[13] As she compellingly argues, salvation memory positions Fujimori as "the economic and physical savior of Peru." In contrast, "human rights memory" has a completely different point of departure: "The 'human rights memory' narrative, held by many human rights groups and organizations of affected family members, does not portray the end of the internal conflict as a victory over terrorism but situates the violence as an extension of ongoing legacies of social and political inequalities of which Shining Path was a symptom and on which Shining Path was able to build its movement."[14]

Dominant publics that remain resistant and hostile to a holistic discussion about the internal conflict endorse a "salvation memory" narrative because it renders state accountability mute. In contrast, counterpublics foster human rights memory that can draw an explicit or implicit link to decolonial feminism, which does not absolve legacies of racism and misogyny. The children of parents and community members affected by wars and social unrest inherit the traumas of their communities, parents, and grandparents.[15] These painful generational legacies (or ghosts) do not somehow disappear because Congress passed the right law or through the incarceration of abusive and corrupt people.

A decolonial feminist perspective emphasizes the political and imaginative power and potential of human rights memory. Addressing injustice outside of the formal arena of the state means that solutions will not come via patriarchal and masculinist routes. If we take as a given that governments will disappoint or take longer than needed to do the "right thing" (whatever that might be in terms of policy), then it merits understanding that during the period of transitional justice activists and artists are not waiting for the governments' response. This is not to suggest that they are forgoing putting demands on their governments, but they are coupling their advocacy and their work with direct engagement or in collaboration with affected communities to advance sociocultural change.

People continue to harbor mistrust of the government and for good reason. Accountability during the postconflict period has been a profoundly challenging process due to the government's attempt to pass immunity laws. In 2010 an Amnesty International report raised concerns about the lack of investigation into killings by police officers, and about a 2007 decree that reformed the penal code and exempted those police officers from being held accountable. Amnesty International also had concerns about what it considered insufficient progress on the recommendations from the CVR, and condemned the minimal progress "made regarding the 1,000 cases of past human rights violations filed with the Public Prosecutor's Office since 2003." It noted that those cases that had moved forward through the courts often "yielded disappointing results." The report also expressed serious concern about the lack of financial support given to the government body established in 2006 "to create a record of victims of human rights violations during the two decades of internal armed conflict so that they could claim reparation," since in November 2010 that government office had to temporarily suspend its work due to insufficient funds.[16]

As mentioned earlier, the transitional justice toolkit involves several important mechanisms—from investigations and eventual criminal trials to reparations programs. These are formalized processes in which states engage as part of their postconflict rebuilding efforts and to restore their international reputations. The most promising period of Peruvian transitional justice was from 2001–2003 under former president Alejandro Toledo, the first Indigenous president (who has also been charged with corruption and is currently in prison awaiting trial). Presidential administrations since 2003 have been less willing to directly engage in the CVR report's recommendations because of their role. For example, Alan García, who was president from 1985 to 1990 and elected again in 2003 had been implicated during the early years of the internal conflict. García shockingly committed suicide in his home on April 17, 2019, as he was being arrested for corruption charges.

Although the formal and legal processes of transitional justice are paramount when striving for responsibility and accountability, exploring the sociocultural aspects means looking past or beyond laws, because they too often reflect the interests of the dominant public or of those in power and can also be discriminatory—even if those laws are being adopted at the time of a country's transition. Any rebuilding of society must involve both small and grand gestures of human connection (from speaking to and trusting one's neighbors to building a museum focused on the perspective of those directly affected to learn from the trauma) to enact sociocultural transformation to address the root causes of internal conflicts or wars. Further, a decolonial feminist perspective of transitional justice affirms Indigenous-based cosmologies or worldviews that promote respect for all living entities, including mountains, waters, and forests. A decolonial feminist perspective on transitional justice is not about an investment in liberalism, and thus reform, but rather about genuine transformation. This perspective considers the various forms of oppression and repression that sustain inequality through the maintenance of a status quo that benefits elites.

In a class I teach on contemporary Perú, I facilitate an exercise called "The Roots of War and Peace" developed by The Advocates for Human Rights in Minneapolis.[17] I employ my mediocre artistic skills to draw a tree and ask students to brainstorm on the effects of the Peruvian internal conflict, which are the "fruits of the tree." Examples include trauma, human rights violations, the disappearance of activists and other community members, violence, and fear. Next, students are asked to consider the trunk, to identify the different factors that led to the fruit, specifically in terms of beliefs and programs or policies. Here students discuss displacement, exclusion, land grabs, neglect, and social inequalities. Then we arrive at the roots, where students identify the sources of the social problems that led to the internal conflict. These include poverty, racism, gender oppression, extreme neglect and alienation, colonialism, lack of respect, and antagonism toward human rights standards. By the time we get to the step of identifying the roots, all of us can see that the success of transitional justice rests on grappling with the roots first and foremost.

The image of the tree can also serve as a metaphor for an incident that feminist political scientist Pascha Bueno-Hansen, also a child of the Peruvian diaspora, writes about in her book.[18] She opens the book with a description of talking to a mother whose daughter was taken in 1995. This mother grieved for her daughter, who is now part of the Peruvian disappeared. Eventually two neighborhood women approached them to tell them that someone had broken the branches of a tree in their community garden. Upset about this disregard for the tree that had just started to bloom, the mother said to Bueno-Hansen, "What kind of person would do that, break the branches of the trees in this nice garden?" The mother concluded that whoever had done such a disrespectful act must have "lots of anger inside." What is being broken off here is a recognition of the effects of the internal conflict (the human rights violations, and the widespread violence and trauma associated with the disappeared or victims). As Bueno-Hansen and the mother left their meeting spot on that day, the effects of the internal conflict were being figuratively removed from a tree that, for a brief moment, had represented some beauty and pleasure in an Ayacucho community ravaged by violence.[19] As Bueno-Hansen argues, "The underlying linear temporal logic of transitional justice alleges the ability to divide a past filled with atrocity from a present based on peace."[20] Heeding Bueno-Hansen's concern about a loss of vital knowledge in a linear frame, the research discussed here also seeks to challenge this divide between past and present, and to envision a transition or transitional justice that grapples with these legacies. Thus, a decolonial version of transitional justice is about transformation. Governments and the political winds change, but the community, and the need to achieve coexistence (both with other humans and with other species), remain.

The human rights discourse is particularly fraught in Perú because it has been coupled with the ideology of the leftist guerrilla movements that claimed to be about the rights of the poor but were actually invested in overthrowing the government through anarchy. One of the most important human rights organizations during the internal conflict (and arguably today as well) is the Coordinadora Nacional de Derechos Humanos (National Human Rights Coordinating Body). Several human rights organizations are responsible for its founding, including La Asociación Pro Derechos Humanos (APRODEH, The Association for Human Rights). Both organizations formed in the early 1980s. The general approach of human rights organizations at the time of the early years of the internal conflict was to criticize the state's actions, as opposed to the actions of the leftist guerrilla groups, because of the state's responsibility for upholding human rights (as a signatory to numerous international conventions). However, this approach, which followed the traditional expectations of human rights organizations internationally, cost them dearly in the long run in terms of reputation. Their delayed response to denouncing the insurgency groups Sendero Luminoso and the MRTA meant these human rights organizations became perceived by government officials and other elites as "terrorist sympathizers"—a perception that such organizations and human rights activists continue to reckon with today. Human rights organizations remain a frequent target of the political right wing, and it is not uncommon for their websites to be hacked or their buildings to be vandalized, which I discuss in Chapter 1.

The work of human rights activists and artists in Perú (and around the world) is embattled when we foreground the intersection of global capitalism and global white supremacy. Taken together, capitalism and white supremacy have created a citizenship hierarchy throughout the world that reflects the unfortunate sociocultural realities of racism, exclusion, and marginalization. Latin American studies scholar Paulo Drinot provides the historical context for this intersection in the formation of the Peruvian nation-state through the implementation of industrialization projects of the early twentieth century, and anthropologist Fabiana Li, also a child of the Peruvian diaspora, offers a contemporary analysis of mining conflicts in the country that brings this intersection to the present.[21] Mining is "principally a foreign business," conducted with companies from China, the United States, Canada, Switzerland, and Australia.[22] Moreover, funding for social programs and social policies in the country is supported by the "fiscal contribution of extractive industries," consequently positioning the government's interest in preserving their investment, and opening up sectors of biodiverse lands, such as the Amazon, for private industries.[23]

US political scientist Rebecca Root states, "It would be unfair to lay all the blame [for the shortcomings of the transitional justice period] on the state. The problem lies in part with the Peruvian public."[24] For Root, the public remains largely unwilling to grapple with the depth of the human rights atrocities that occurred as part of the counterinsurgency strategies of Perú in the 1980s and 1990s. It is far easier to blame as the sole culprits the extreme leftist guerrilla groups and anyone (fairly or unfairly) associated with them.[25] Even after all these years, too much of the mainstream public in Lima remains largely reluctant to condemn the state for its role in the internal conflict. Moreover, the same public sector predominately supports the state's ongoing use of deadly force against Andean peasant protesters in mining conflicts.²⁶ Further, the 2021 elections in which the leftist Pedro Castillo won over the hard-right candidate Keiko Fujimori with a mere 50.13 percent of the vote underscores that there is still an incredible divide in Perú.²⁷ In the Epilogue, I discuss President Castillo's epic downfall at the end of 2022.

Decolonizing human rights involves multiple steps, not all of which can be explored in this book or with the research I have done, including unsettling the people-centric idea of the "human" in human rights. I take great inspiration from Indigenous cosmologies that problematize the narrow conceptualization of the "human" or of humanity, as if somehow the forest, the water, the land, and the mountains were not living beings. Though I draw from decolonial approaches to transitional justice, I do so recognizing that my engagement here is somewhat limited, as decolonization is an ongoing and emergent process, always moving into the future.²⁸

Dominant Publics, Counterpublics, and the Formation of the Peruvian Nation-State

Dominant publics and counterpublics contribute to a "multiplicity of publics" that are both competing and conflictual.²⁹ But what exactly do the terms "dominant publics" and "counterpublics" mean? My use of "dominant publics" refers to the spheres of elite spaces in which the power to maintain the status quo of social inequalities resides. This power is political, economic, and discursive. Dominant publics in the context of Peruvian transitional justice are not just entities such as transnational corporations, the government, political parties, and other publicly elected officials, but also include the discursive terrain or logic that seeks to invalidate, systematically erase, ignore, disregard, reimagine, and/or rewrite the complicated narrative regarding the internal conflict itself.

Counterpublics are essential to participatory democratic politics because this space can be "understood as critical oppositional forces within the society of late capitalism."³⁰ Thus, counterpublics represent nonelite or nonprivileged spaces of opposition that reflect "differential consciousness" based on politics, social positions, worldviews, and so forth. When "subordinated groups become subjects rather than objects of discourse," they belong to a counterpublic sphere, and therefore the counterpublic "marks both a heuristic for critique and a particular kind of entity engaged in real-world political practice."³¹

This book is specifically interested in Lima-based counterpublics for human rights and the manner in which they contest tiers of citizenship. As Lima, the capital, remains at the epicenter of sociopolitical power, a focus on what is happening there is critical. I examine the formation of human rights counterpublics in three key arenas: public art and community education projects, as well as their related collectives, when applicable; public commemoration events by activists about the internal conflict; and domestic labor advocacy efforts on behalf of and working with displaced communities to undo histories of abuse and exploitation. As they seek to foster sociocultural changes, these human rights counterpublics are contributing to transitional justice efforts in a meaningful way that is distinct from the legal realm.

These counterpublics are an essential component to building a human rights culture in which tiers of citizenship can be undone. The human rights counterpublics discussed in my research are striving to cultivate what I refer to as "transformative memory" that draws, explicitly and implicitly, from decolonial feminism. Providing one of the most nuanced portraits of Sendero Luminoso in his extensive research, the late Carlos Iván Degregori underscored how the "refusal to recognize what happened" during the internal conflict by segments of Peruvian society is "perhaps a habit of repressing subaltern memories."[32] In addition, a 2013 national poll taken on the ten-year anniversary of the final Comisión de la Verdad y Reconciliación report revealed that only 34 percent of Peruvians even knew about the CVR and its corresponding report, suggesting that despite its widespread public outreach efforts, the majority of Peruvians have not heard of the CVR.[33] The problem then is two-fold: some who have heard about the CVR are unwilling to engage with the report's findings and others remain unaware of its very existence.

Human Rights Counterpublics in Perú exposes the exclusionary realities embedded within legal citizenship due to a range of social factors shaped by race, ethnicity, class, gender, sexuality, geography, language, and education status.[34] National legal citizenship did not offer protection for the largely Andean communities who needed security—security from state and insurgent terror but also from economic precarity and exclusion. The idea of tiers speaks to scales, and the scalar model of citizenship recognizes that these levels of citizenship are based not on equality but on a sociopolitical-elite hierarchy. The lower tier of citizenship, the citizen-others, is meant to benefit the upper tier, the citizen-elites.

Perhaps it seems odd to use the term "citizen" in a project that draws from decolonial feminism. Citizenship, after all, is a colonial marker throughout the world. Yet I do not approach the category of citizen from the juridical or legal viewpoint. The case of Perú underscores that legal status is a farce when it comes to protection from the state because societal elites could not care less about what happens to legal citizens who live on the margins of society. I conceptualize the category of citizen from the sociopolitical realm. Thus, I refer to a citizen as an inhabitant, as the steward of a place in the world for a certain period of time. In this way, I then consider how a decolonial engagement with the category of citizen means that it has nothing to do with legal status, recognizing that the imposition of status is fundamentally flawed, since it is rooted in exclusion. By being stewards, people are accountable to one another and for one another, mandating a response to a sociopolitical-elite hierarchy that leaves certain communities perpetually disenfranchised.

Migration and citizenship studies scholar Bridget Anderson offers useful citizen categories with which to analyze the sociopolitical-elite hierarchy: "failed citizen," "good citizen," and "tolerated citizen." Following this typology, Peruvian Indigenous peoples would be considered the "failed citizens," and activists and artists the "tolerated citizens," though these categories are in no way mutually exclusive, because one can be both simultaneously. The "failed citizen" refers to the criminal, the prisoner, the poor, the teenage mother, and the citizens who fail to live up to the purported image of the "good citizen"—the law-abiding, tax-paying, heterosexual individual who is deemed meritorious of citizenship because of their morally indisputable good standing.[35] Anderson argues that a "failed citizen" can be a "tolerated citizen" who has some of the qualities of a "good citizen." A "tolerated citizen," namely an activist, criticizes the state and government. A social justice activist could be a tolerated citizen in a country that does not imprison political dissidents.

Applying these citizen categories to the formation of the Peruvian state reveals the centrality of racism targeting Indigenous communities. As Paulo Drinot argues, the goal of the formation of the Peruvian state was "the de-Indianization of Perú," since Indigenous peoples (and African-descendants) were not deemed worthy of national citizenship because their lifeways represented a past that elites saw as "backward."[36] As Drinot contends, the foundation of the nation-state of Perú was built on racism and patriarchy that relegate Indigenous peoples to the realm of "failed citizens" because these marginalized communities were not invested in the industrialization projects of the elites in the early twentieth century. The objective of these industrialization projects was to portray a "civilized" Perú to global elites, and to transform Andean citizens into the right type of citizens, ones that state elites believe earned or merited citizenship because they advanced capitalist interests.[37]

The CVR's final report reinforces these citizen categories, citing the legacies of racism and misogyny as contributing factors that led to the longevity and brutality of the internal conflict against "failed" or "tolerated" citizens. Emotional public testimonies given by women during the CVR investigation revealed extensive gender-based and sexual violence,[38] a topic powerfully explored online by the Quipu Project.[39] The CVR process and its final report brought forty-seven cases for prosecution, two of which were rape cases.[40]

Through their political actions, activism, and commitment to social justice, the human rights counterpublics in Perú call attention to two critical failures of dominant publics. First, widespread state oppression and repression has not resulted, nor will ever result, in "the de-Indianization of Peru," to borrow from Drinot. This "sanitizing" or "civilizing" project is a failed one that dates back to the colonial period. Second, the "transitional justice toolkit," to borrow a term from Root, that prioritizes legal change reveals the deficiencies or "false hope" of dominant institutions. Institutional reform is not about transformation, and reform can lead to new forms of repression.[41]

Hence, I argue that the human rights counterpublics discussed in this research are creating a "transformative memory." Drawing from decolonial feminism, *transformative memory* is about agitating for societal changes by directly confronting legacies of repression that have resulted in tiers of citizenship. Transformation will be much deeper and more meaningful than anything reform could offer communities, as reformation leaves too many societal structures intact. And it is through decolonial feminism that we can begin to reconceptualize human rights—its multifaceted meanings, promise, and limitations—in order to remember and reimagine Perú itself.

About Methodology and Self-Reflexivity

Today the Miraflores district has blossomed into a real tourist destination, with eateries, cafés, large hotel chains (such as the Marriott), vibrant parades put on by Wong supermarkets to celebrate Peruvian independence, and an expensive outdoor mall called Larcomar overlooking the Pacific Ocean. Returning to Perú in the summer of 2008 felt entirely different from the many previous trips I had taken there with my family and my own solo trip in 2003 to conduct dissertation research on antiracist feminist activism in the Americas.[42] In 2008 my research trip involved traveling on my own with my then three-year-old daughter and renting our own apartment. The added identity of parent—solo parent, since my husband could not travel with me on any of my research trips to Lima—created new ways of engaging the research process and the subject matter. The multiple hats I was wearing at that time—researcher, parent, transnational family member—meant that the research was going to be carried out differently than in 2003, and my parental responsibilities would be first and foremost. It also felt different because my research lens would be squarely focused on Perú rather than on comparing activist engagements in other countries, as in my previous book. I felt ready to confront the haunting and complex legacies of the internal conflict I had managed to avoid from a sociopolitical and geographical distance. Perú has always felt like another home base for me, which is perhaps part of the reason I felt it important to travel there with my daughter so that she could meet our extended family. And yet I needed to be mindful of what I might miss as a researcher. When things start to feel familiar, the "feminist curiosity," as the US political scientist Cynthia Enloe calls it, can wane.[43]

This book relies on qualitative methodologies to tell the story of contesting tiers of citizenship and human rights counterpublics. I was in Lima conducting dissertation research in 2003 when the CVR released its final report after a two-year investigation. The CVR heard hundreds of brutal testimonies, analyzed the data collected, offered recommendations for reconciliation, and produced a report that put the realities of the internal conflict front and center in the news. Even though I was not in Lima to specifically research the CVR report, I had an interest in the transitional justice process, knowing that I would be engaging with it in some capacity in the future.

Like my relationship with the United States, my relationship with this land of Perú is fraught and lovely. I feel a familial connection to this special place. Its stunning beauty captivates me, its pain and trauma haunt me, and its political life jars me. By focusing on a country in which my ancestors lived, that is the birthplace of my parents, and that has such a distinct history and sociopolitical context in Latin America, I inadvertently found myself reckoning with my own questions: What if my parents had never left? What would my life have become? Sometimes I wonder if those nagging questions have led me to this research project.

Learning about Perú from antiracist feminist activists during my dissertation research in the early 2000s has undoubtedly shaped this current project. The lingering intellectual and political research questions focused on human rights activism at the intersection of racism and patriarchy that remained after I had finished my dissertation research have led to this project. This "feminist curiosity" has led me to ask, how does Perú move away from human rights violations and toward human rights realizations? Utopic and indeed hopeful, this persistent question guides a program of research today in which activist visions are leading us into a future based on dignity, equity, respect, and love (see the Epilogue).

As discussed previously, I started the primary data collection for this project by first approaching La Casa de Panchita. I described myself as a human rights scholar-activist, the daughter of Peruvian immigrants, and referenced the BBC Mundo article from which I heard about the organization.

When I arrived in Lima in June 2008, I went to Panchita every day that summer and again in 2010 and 2011 to engage in participant observation and conduct both formal and informal interviews. I would sit in the main lounge area and talk to the women who were seeking its services and advice. I have extensive field notes describing the comings and goings of people in the organization, from staff to domestic worker clients. I observed the organization's all-day, twice weekly law workshops. One summer I also observed a cooking workshop. The purpose of the law workshops was to explain to prospective employees their legal rights, which I discuss in detail in Chapter 3. Other workshops, including cooking and first aid training, helped women gain skills that would appeal to prospective employers. I would often invite women to lunch during the training breaks and hear the stories about how they became domestic workers and about the abuse they endured in this line of work. We discussed how they had learned about Panchita—which was almost always by word of mouth—and what they hoped to gain from participating in the workshops.

Panchita also offers tutorial programs aimed at young girls living in the outskirts of Lima. The staff engages in on-the-ground outreach and advocacy, meaning they go door to door, or literally shack to shack, in the community and talk to families about the importance of their daughters' education. Rosa, the staff person doing this on-the-ground advocacy, invited me to join her one day, an experience I will never forget. Traveling in microbuses from Miraflores, where I had rented an apartment, to San Juan de Miraflores, where Panchita had established the girls' tutorial program, made evident the striking class disparity between the two Miraflores. Even though San Juan de Miraflores was just six miles away, it felt like a different world, and I was able to observe Panchita's work inside the organization as well as outside in the community. During my time at Panchita, in addition to the opportunities to engage in participant observation, I was able to interview the executive director, a staff person, and several domestic workers who participated in the workshops.

During less chaotic periods of research, a staff person asked if I would look for possible grant sources. I usually did this when I arrived home at night, and would make a list for the Panchita staff. Also, I translated one of the organization's substantial progress reports into English for a funder in Denmark. As a fundamental of feminist methodological practice, I knew that I needed to reciprocate in some way for having access to the organization and for the opportunity, the privilege, to talk to domestic workers.

Starting in 2013 and on through the conclusion of my primary data collection in 2015, I expanded my research to more directly engage the aftermath of the internal conflict by immersing myself in commemoration events, whether it be observing scholar-activist presentations about memory studies at local bookshops or those organized by the Memory Group of the Institute of Peruvian Studies (Instituto de Estudios Peruanos), or attending an August 2015 conference in Lima called "ENCUENTRO: Cultura, Arte y Cambio Social" (ENCOUNTER: Culture, Art, and Social Change) at which some of the artists I had interviewed were giving presentations. In a very emotionally moving experience in 2013, I assisted APRODEH with a commemoration event honoring a disappeared person at a memorial called El Ojo Que Llora (The Eye that Cries). The woman and the two daughters who gathered to honor a husband and father named Jorge wore their pain on their sleeves even twenty years after the disappearance, reminders that sometimes trauma and wounds never heal. I also helped with another less emotional event in 2015 in which nearby school children (the postmemory generation) came to learn about the memorial.

For this research I interviewed staff members from the two most important human rights organizations in Perú—APRODEH and Coordinadora Nacional de Derechos Humanos—and interviewed a staff person from the Ministry of Education responsible for intercultural education in Indigenous communities, as well as a teacher at an alternative school based on a human rights curriculum, and the lawyer of the Human Rights Division of Flora Tristan, one of the oldest women's organizations in Lima. The lawyer worked with a coalition of community activists determined to keep the CVR alive. I interviewed artists who are part of the Museo Itinerante Arte por la Memoria collective as well as another artist collective called HAMBRE. I was also able to view the Museo Itinerante exhibit at the 2015 conference in Lima mentioned above.

During my various research trips, I would also visit *Yuyanapaq*, the curated collection of photos that accompany the CVR's report. The Museo Nacional housed the exhibit for a number of years, with controversies ensuing about its location once the Lugar de la Memoria, la Tolerancia y la Inclusión Social (LUM) opened in 2015. These photos expose the capacity for cruelty; and a decolonial feminist analysis of the photos in the exhibit shows how a "salvation memory" narrative emerges by largely (nearly exclusively) focusing on the actions of one group in the images—Sendero Luminoso. The Museo Nacional is a state museum, and so it would be in the state's interest to carefully curate a photo exhibit about the internal conflict. But a decolonial feminist analysis asks for a deeper exploration of the ideologies embedded within the Peruvian nation-state than is on display here, especially with regard to the portrayal of social justice activists such as María Elena Moyano, whose sister is a Fujimorista (referring to a strong supporter of President Fujimori) member of Congress.[44]

I also wanted to visit the Lugar de la Memoria—or Place of Memory—in 2015, right before it officially opened. LUM was supposed to have been opened when I arrived in 2015 but the opening had been delayed for months. Unfortunately, LUM opened after I left Perú, but I was able to interview one of the former directors—Denise Ledgard—who was suddenly and unexpectedly ousted during my time in Lima. My interview with her offers insights into the messy politics of opening LUM.

In 2015 I also had a chance to see *Sin Título* performed by one of the oldest theater troupes in Latin America, Yuyachkani, a Quechua word meaning "I am thinking, I am remembering." This incredible performance took place at a local theater, where the audience was first invited to walk through a display room in a side hallway before entering the main theater space. This side room contained hundreds of magazines, images, short videos, and other items from the internal conflict period. It was a space where viewers could go back in time to better understand the performance they were about to witness. Dr. Salomón Lerner, the president of the CVR, described the performance as a "symbolic" form of reparations: "[The Yuyachkani performances] . . . contributed to the fostering of an apt context in which to carry out the process [of preparing for the public hearings]—to the solemnity and ceremony appropriate to an act of symbolic reparations to the victims."[45]

Lastly, in July 2015 I also interviewed Dr. Lerner in his university office at Pontificia Universidad Católica del Perú and Pablo Zavala of Instituto Peruano de Educacíon en Derechos Humanos y la Paz about their human rights popular education curriculum. The Lerner interview was especially significant, given that he was the president of the CVR and has been on the receiving end of some intense slander by Fujimoristas. He also offers an insider's perspective on the challenges facing the CVR process and the cultural and systemic apathy of Peruvian society. As part of this research, I also collected and analyzed ten years of newspaper coverage that referenced the internal conflict, from 2003 to 2013, with 2013 being the ten-year anniversary of the publication of the CVR's report, as mentioned above.

My overall research seeks to understand transformative memory and the different realms of engaged work by human rights counterpublics.[46] By relying on an array of qualitative data sources, this research sets out to decipher the struggle for justice. To that end, Peruvian transitional justice efforts remain incomplete and in process; they remain frustrated by a disinterested dominant public yet inspired by human rights counterpublics that pursue justice even in the midst of great political uncertainty.

Overview of the Chapters

Dr. Lerner said to President Toledo at the 2003 ceremony in Ayacucho marking the end of the commission's work and rendering its report public for the first time: "The report we hand in contains a double outrage: that of massive murder, disappearance and torture; and that of [the] indolence, incompetence and indifference of those who could have stopped this humanitarian catastrophe but didn't."[47] All these years later, what is clearly at stake is how to remember the conflict and how to unfold an "active memory" in order to heal the past and grapple with future injustice. How can a culture with entrenched social hierarchies, or tiers of citizenship based on race, ethnicity, sexuality, and class, such as that found in Perú, become transformed into a culture that is based (ideally) on the principles of human rights, which includes dignity, respect, and love? I do not have the answers, but I do offer an understanding of how human rights counterpublics are working toward this kind of sociocultural transformation through decolonial feminist praxis. My research strives to better understand the innovative invocations of human rights—as metaphor, as analytic, and as a call to action—from counterpublics.

The book contains four primary chapters. The first chapter, "Backlash to Building Human Rights Memory," analyzes counterpublic art projects that have been attacked and vandalized since the official end of the internal conflict. This chapter includes a discussion about El Ojo Que Llora (The Eye that Cries) memorial, which is located in a large public park in Lima. Walking the memorial is devastating because it commemorates the dead or the disappeared. The site has been one of massive controversy and a prime target for those who are unsettled by efforts to hold the state accountable. Chapter 1 underscores how transitional justice art is a provocation with the intent to rupture the racist and patriarchal complacency that facilitated the longevity of the internal conflict in the first place. I apply a decolonial feminist analysis to select artworks in order to contextualize the possibility of a democratic project of inclusivity within an atmosphere of tangible and visible human rights backlash.

Chapter 2, "Memory Recovery through Art and Education," is about how art and public education curricula are fundamental to transformative memory. The project of memory making following an internal conflict and during the transitional justice period reveals insights into the politics of social location and the political stakes of remembrance. Which memory is to be preserved for the national and international record? Whose perspective is mainstreamed and whose is suppressed or dismissed by the state and/or the elites complicit in the violence? These projects are meant for those who are open to dealing with the roots of the internal conflict. These creative outlets inspire difficult conversations that reach new audiences.

The focus of Chapter 3, "*No Somos Invisibles*: Domestic Workers and La Casa de Panchita," is about how, with support from this organization, domestic workers could assert their rights as citizens with inherent dignity. Many of the women I interviewed came from geographic locations directly in the crosshairs of the internal conflict, and their relocation to Lima has led to isolation and exploitation. When domestic workers come to Panchita, they become equipped with a network of support that provides knowledge about how to navigate the terrain of power between employer and employee. Panchita reframes domestic work as skilled labor, an important shift from how this labor was seen prior to the passage of the Domestic Workers Law in 2003. Panchita's advocates, together with the domestic workers who seek their support, have formed a human rights counterpublic that is trying to eradicate entrenched racist and sexist views about Andean, Indigenous, and campesina women and their labor.

Chapter 4 addresses how the formation of human rights counterpublics is about envisioning a new Perú. Titled "Ghosts, Hauntings, and Unsettling the Tiers of Citizenship," this final chapter seeks to disrupt the normalization of citizenship tiers and contends that these human rights counterpublics are responding to a history of pain, trauma, and woundedness that has barely been acknowledged. They are dancing with ghosts and illuminating a path toward reconciliation. Analyzing ten years of newspaper media coverage to trace the public narrative about the internal conflict in the decade following the release of the CVR's final report, this chapter underscores that a decolonial light needs to shine to break through an impasse in which nothing changes, to set the conditions in which transformative memory can occur. After all, how will postmemory generations, the generations not directly affected by the internal conflict, respond to Perú's complicated history as the country's future leaders? This question has added urgency, because after Abimael Guzmán was captured in 1992 and Sendero Luminoso lost its power, an offshoot of Sendero, Movimiento por la Amnistía y los Derechos Fundamentales (known as MOVADEF), has emerged in Perú that deeply troubles human rights activists today.

In the Epilogue, I begin with a discussion of the devasting political situation of 2022 that imploded during the botched coup attempt by former President Castillo, who is imprisoned (at the time of this writing) and awaiting trial, and the insatiable repression and violence that resulted in death and further trauma of Indigenous peoples, with clear echoes of Fujimorismo. The ideology of Fujimorismo embraced by the dominant public is receiving new life. Further, I explore the transnational importance of these radical cultural interventions by Peruvian human rights counterpublics in the context of rising authoritarianism across the globe.

CHAPTER 1

Backlash to Building Human Rights Memory

I remember finally arriving at the Museo Nacional in July 2008 eager to see the *Yuyanapaq* photo exhibition. *Yuyanapaq* is the name of the collection of Comisión de la Verdad y Reconciliación (CVR) photos that remain on permanent display on the fifth floor of Lima's Museo Nacional (until at least 2026). After seeing some of the CVR photos online and in books, I had mixed feelings about the opportunity to finally see them in person. On the elevator ride up to the fifth floor, I took several deep breaths, holding back tears. I would visit *Yuyanapaq* a few times over the course of my research trips to Lima. One visit in particular still stands out for me.

A school group, possibly middle schoolers, was there during one of my visits. These young people, born after the years of the internal conflict, are considered the postmemory generation. When I saw this group of young people, I remember feeling hopeful that perhaps this visit to the museum would be illuminating to them as a pedagogical experience, helping them realize that they had inherited a legacy of political violence that would be important for them to understand. This hope was short-lived.

I made eye contact and smiled at one of the adults; she returned the gesture and started to gather the kids into small groups to tour the exhibit with the other adult chaperones. As these uniform-wearing kids, some with cameras in hand, were getting ready to head in, I entered the venue ahead of them. I would run into this group several times during that visit. I noticed after several minutes that their energy level stayed elevated. I thought that the rapid talking and laughing would subside once they started to take in the pictures. I was wrong. In one of the exhibit rooms, with photos of an Andean woman in despair and military personnel in the background, the kids pointed and laughed. Then they started to take selfies and other pictures with bunny ears hand gestures, with the exhibit photographs in the background. I started to feel uncomfortable, wondering why the adults did not stop this disrespectful and disruptive behavior. Did the kids' jovial behavior bother the adult chaperones as it did me, or were they just overwhelmed with keeping everyone together, which can happen on school field trips? I left that day feeling upset and confused. If this is the reaction of some postmemory youth to images of the internal conflict, is there any reason to be hopeful about the country's future?

I happened to have interviews scheduled with human rights artists after this incident occurred, so I thought it an opportune time to add a question about what my interviewees thought about my museum experience, in which rather than conveying empathy and compassion, the young people had mocked the pain and despair on display. Jorge, an activist-artist of Japanese descent, said, "It is true that there is a majority in the country that is indifferent toward their neighbor's suffering. I think that the ability to feel empathy is being lost, the ability to put oneself in the other's place, in the other's shoes. This, I think, has to do with the capitalist system, which is not just an economic system but a civilizing one; it creates civilization. [And] at the same time, and the CVR has already said this, [the internal conflict] takes place in a deeply racist society, where some citizens seem to be worth less than others."[1] Jorge's assertion that capitalism is a civilizing project that has resulted in a fragmented society dates back to the early formation of the state.[2] Paulo Drinot contends that Perú's quest to be an industrialized nation was as much about Eurocentric cultural aspirations as it was about economics. Noting that Peruvian elites felt that "industrialization had a dark side" because of the promotion of "subversive ideologies" that led to the social unrest happening in Europe and North America at the time, Drinot compellingly shows how racial and gender logics undergirded the elite imagination of what Perú could become *without Indigenous peoples*. This elite imagination harkens back to a period of colonial genocide throughout the Americas region. As Drinot asserts, "two Perus" emerged during the period of industrialization that was at its core about de-Indianization, emboldening a colonial project that sought to systematically erase indigeneity in all its forms—the communities, the culture, the lifeways, the cosmologies, and so forth.

When I told my museum story to Mauricio, Jorge's friend and artistic collaborator, he responded, "It's sad, isn't it? Well, the Indigenous person, the Quechua-speaking person, is a sort of laughingstock in Lima," and added that the "distance" those young people exhibited in their reaction was not only about "the distance from the experience of the conflict, but it's also [about] the *campesina*, the woman who is [viewed as] a laughingstock in her everyday life."[3] For both Jorge and Mauricio, the young people's reaction was not surprising, though it did sadden them that so little seems to have been learned from the CVR report. Though they consider the CVR report flawed or rather incomplete, they do regard it as an important document and as research to defend. Mauricio even had a role in producing an abbreviated version of the CVR report in English that included his artwork.[4]

As artist-activists (or artivists), Jorge and Mauricio are addressing the twin pillar plagues of Peruvian society—racism and capitalism—that have resulted in a fractured and disconnected society and fosters a toxic space in which the reactions of the postmemory generation at the museum are not seen as shocking. The photography from the CVR report is intended to inspire the production of memory for the postmemory generation; yet the response by these young people in this singular case reveals just how challenging building human rights memory can be, leading one to question the purpose of and the audience for such memory-making projects.

The reaction of the postmemory generation that I witnessed is representative of a larger societal backlash by the dominant public to the creation of human rights memory that undergirds the context in which artist-activists are creating their art projects. The focus in this chapter is on two public art projects that have been harmed by those who objected to their meaning. The overt display of power shown by the targeting and attempted destruction of public art indicates that something sinister is happening in Perú, and specifically in Lima. How should we understand the resistance to the memories being conveyed or provoked by public art projects? Through the backlash against human rights memory we can better understand the complicated terrain and process for transformative memory making. These public art projects serve as a method of fostering unspoken difficult dialogues, revealing a schism between empathy and hostility that unleashes the power to suppress memories.

The process of memory making through art projects involves curating incredibly fraught memories.[5] As Erica Lehrer and Cynthia Milton state:

> We may legitimately ask how much—and what kind—of debate and contention we want, recognizing that the curation of difficult knowledge can exacerbate conflict, or keep wounds traumatically open when they might otherwise heal. Yet curating "reconciliation" risks other erasures, neglects, and negations, potentially inflicting further harm by silencing those living with scars, still-open wounds, or ongoing injustice. There is a need for curatorial work that can both reveal and contain tensions,

highlighting the ways that aggrieved parties live in "contentious coexistence" in the aftermath of violence, while also creating spaces for more robust "dissensual community" to emerge.[6]

The "curation of difficult knowledge" through the production of art must then consider how to navigate the tensions between the dominant public and the counterpublic while also recognizing that "difficult knowledge" is not singular or universal and is linked to social location. As Elizabeth Jelin argues, "Silences or hidden ethnic, cultural, or gender dimensions come to light in the course of the unfolding of violent conflicts and in their aftermaths."[7]

The two public art projects discussed in this chapter emanate from the counterpublic.[8] One is a mural by the famous political artist Victor Delfín outside the office of the Asociación Pro Derechos Humanos (Association for Human Rights, or APRODEH) depicting a mosaic of past and future Perú. The other is the memorial El Ojo Que Llora (The Eye That Cries) representing lives lost during the internal conflict. I selected these two art projects because the counterpublic played a role in supporting their creation and because they are in publicly accessible spaces: APRODEH is based in a local neighborhood and the organization asked Delfín to paint the mural; El Ojo Que Llora is located in a large public park in Lima and relied on community volunteers for its development. Reading the artworks through a decolonial feminist lens as well as feminist intersectionality illustrates that transformative memory is possible when a willingness exists to engage with the multiple meanings of counterpublic art. This engagement leaves the participant changed, setting them on a road to social change and an understanding that the status quo cannot continue. I proceed first with some background about the internal conflict in Perú.

Background on the Peruvian Internal Conflict

The two-decade internal conflict should be primarily seen as having two time periods: 1980–1992 and 1992–2000, with the break in 1992 resulting from Fujimori's self-coup on April 5, 1992. During the self-coup, Fujimori dissolved the Congress and ruled the country by executive decrees. Perú stayed in this state of political chaos for many months, until new congressional elections took place on November 22, 1992, when Fujimori's political party, Cambio 90, won the majority of seats and subsequently rewrote the Constitution the following year so that Fujimori could run for an unprecedented third term.

In the first time period, 1980–1992, Perú had undergone some of the most brutal events associated with the internal conflict. The country was coming off years of military rule with the election of Fernando Belaúnde Terry from 1980 to 1985 (who had been president before, from 1963 to 1968 until a coup in 1968) and then a transition of democratic power to Alan García (1985–1990). Neither Belaúnde nor García could respond to the growing insurgency, and both administrations severely worsened economic conditions in the country. Fujimori was then democratically elected in 1990, beating García's reelection bid.

On May 17, 1980, "five hooded Shining Path guerrillas entered the voter registration office in Chuschi, a village of mostly Quechua-speaking peasants in the Andean department of Ayacucho. Known as *Senderistas*, these Shining Path members tied up the registrar on duty and set the registry and ballot boxes ablaze. This event, known as the *Inicio de la Lucha Armada* (the start of the internal conflict), symbolically ignited the Shining Path guerrilla insurrection,"[9] making Chuschi the symbolic birthplace of the insurgency and a "rebel stronghold" for several years. Chuschi is a remote community of just over one hundred people who were mostly self-sufficient, surviving off the land in this fertile agricultural zone. After the ballot box burning and the official declaration of war against the state, the Shining Path started to engage in its war of terror throughout Ayacucho, which means "Corner of the Dead" in Quechua.[10] The group eventually spread its reach throughout the territory. Sendero Luminoso successfully recruited hundreds of people living in the Andes whom the state had virtually ignored.

Three years after the declaration of war in Chuschi, Sendero Luminoso came to Huaychao, a former hacienda. An isolated and remote area with about fifty families, Huaychao is considered the birthplace of counterinsurgency. Here eight Senderistas came in "chanting revolutionary slogans and carrying the red Communist flag."[11] Sendero Luminoso was under the impression that this village supported them, but these eight people were taken to a room, beaten, and then killed. As word spread about the killing of Senderistas in the area, "the proliferation of peasant counterinsurgency militias" (known as *rondas campesinas*) began.[12] The response by Sendero Luminoso was to destroy these Andean villages and instill a level of fear throughout the valley never seen before. So the killings of Senderistas in Huaychao and the subsequent formation of *rondas campesinas* meant that widespread and generational devastation was on its way. The response came in April 1983, with Sendero Luminoso's massacre at Lucanamarca, which left eighty people dead (including women, children, and elders).

In an interview in 1988, Abimael Guzmán, the main leader of Sendero Luminoso, said, "We responded decisively with an overwhelming action: Lucanamarca. Neither they nor we will forget it, of course, because they saw a response that had not been imagined. There more than 80 were annihilated, that is the reality. . . . The main thing was for us to strike a massive blow and reprimand them, making them understand that they were dealing with another kind of people's combatants, that they were not dealing with the kind of combatants that operated earlier, that is what they understand."[13] Dubbed "the Interview of the Century" in *El Diario* (the Shining Path's propaganda newspaper), Guzmán was unwavering in his view that those believed to be "collaborating with the government, those who refused submission[,] had to be 'annihilated' in order to channel the masses in the 'riverbed' of revolutionary correctness."[14]

The people of Lima did not really believe the national press reports about Huaychao. How could Andean peasants do such a thing? The other layer to this story is that the military had engaged in a massive counterinsurgency effort three weeks prior to the killings in Huaychao. And the military was known for engaging in entirely indiscriminate killings—put another way, in acts of blind repression. Eight journalists from Lima and Ayacucho went to the area to investigate the killings of the Senderistas, and they, too, along with their guide, ended up dead in Uchuraccay. They were Jorge Sedano, Eduardo de la Piniella, Willy Retto, Pedro Sánchez-Gavidia, Amador García, Jorge Luis Mendivil, Félix Gavilán, Octavio Infante (the journalists), and Juan Argumedo (the guide). To this day, the full story of their murders remains suspect (their bodies were later exhumed), and it remains unknown whether it was the three convicted peasants (Dionisio Morales, Simeón Aucatoma, and Manuel Ccasani) or actually members of the military that killed the journalists and the guide.[15]

The origins of Sendero Luminoso's rise can be traced back to the university in Ayacucho. Led by university intellectuals, including Guzmán, who was a philosophy professor at Ayacucho University, the group did not represent a peasant-centered version of a revolution.[16] Sendero Luminoso's ultimate goal was to achieve "strategic equilibrium," which refers to a "period in the Maoist conception of popular war when defensive guerrilla warfare has achieved a strategic balance with government forces and conflict is transformed into war of positions."[17] Guzmán succeeded in evading capture for nearly thirteen years, contributing to his allure and appeal. A unit branch of the national police that was focused on terrorism eventually captured Guzmán on September 12, 1992.

Even though university intellectuals were the leaders of Sendero Luminoso, its rebels were high school and university students from the area's shantytowns. As Latin American studies scholar Orin Starn wrote, "The new party's internal organisation replicated the colonial stratification of regional society: a privileged elite of white professionals commanded a mass of brown-skinned youth of humble origin."[18] Young people with "personal experience of poverty and racism as children of the dispossessed" were ready to be recruited; they were ready to change their impoverished lives. The military and Sendero Luminoso both engaged in disappearances, tortures, and indiscriminate killings. Ayacuchans paid a deep price during the conflict: "More than three thousand Ayacuchans, most of them impoverished villagers, would be killed in the dirty war in 1984 and 1985 alone," with the bodies of the disappeared never being located.[19]

According to Starn, four themes are prominent in the political ideas of Guzmán, known as "Gonzalo Thought": "the primacy of class struggle," "the need to combat imperialism," "the importance of the vanguard party," and "violence."[20] The centrality of class struggle is obviously aligned with communist thinking. The theme of combating imperialism is seen as a contradiction when compared to the perpetuation of Shining Path's own acts of imperialism, in which support for establishing a vanguard party is coupled with populist propaganda with labels such as *guerra popular* (people's war) and *lucha de masas* (mass struggle), and a "fierce ideology" that "privileged insight and leadership" from those viewed as the leaders, such as Guzmán. The extreme violence exerted by Sendero rebels had to create stark divisions between Senderistas and its opponents. Describing so-called opponents as "'filthy,' 'parasitic,' 'fetid,' 'cancerous,' and 'reptilian' . . . provid[ed] the ideological framework for the murder of hundreds of trade unionists, peasant activists and neighbourhood leaders from other political parties as well as policemen and soldiers. To kill was to cleanse evil. To die was to become a martyr."[21] As stated by a Peruvian Communist Party hymn, "Our chief is Gonzalo / he of brilliant thought and action inspired by Marx, Lenin and Mao / he develops our powerful ideology and brings to a burning world the invincible people's war."[22] Gonzalo Thought attempted a merger of communist ideologies: "The Shining Path was built around the premise that Gonzalo Thought represented, in the words of a follower, the 'highest development of Marxist-Leninist-Mao Zedong Thought.'"[23]

For Starn, Peruvian-style Marxism was actually against Peruvian culture and traditions. That form of Marxism, with its complete focus on universal class struggle, vis-à-vis the Shining Path, should actually be viewed as part of a legacy of imperialism in Latin America. Starn states that in this quest for universal class struggle, the Peruvian Marxism that the Shining Path claimed to embrace actually "flatten[ed] the bumpy distinctiveness of the largest and most diverse of the Andean nations." According to Starn, far from a "Peruvianisation of Marxism," Guzmán actually despised popular Peruvian culture and traditions,[24] and the Shining Path replicated patterns of racial exclusion found in the dominant society or in the dominant public. The Shining Path referred to "Andean villagers as 'Peru's most backward inhabitants' and used racist anti-Asian slurs to attack Fujimori" (who is described as "slitty-eyed" and "reptilian" in *El Diario*).[25]

The outskirts of Lima had also been target sites for the Sendero Luminoso rebels.[26] Sendero Luminoso targeted and frequently killed social justice activists, such as union members or those who supported state-funded social welfare programs. In the view of the terrorist rebels, these activists' willingness to work with the state in any capacity was a problem because they undermined Sendero Luminoso's ultimate mission of achieving anarchy and overthrowing the government. María Elena Moyano—a well-known and respected Afro-Peruvian feminist community leader—was one of the activists targeted by Sendero Luminoso. Members of Sendero Luminoso assassinated her on February 15, 1992, in front of her children and community. To send an even more terrorizing message, they placed bombs beneath her dead body to blow her up and erase her existence entirely. Her death reverberated throughout the community of Villa El Salvador in the outskirts of Lima, and her image has become a symbol of resistance (see Figure 1.1). While Sendero Luminoso was wreaking violence in Lima, the state was targeting those suspected of having an association with Sendero Luminoso in Lima via a notorious secret paramilitary death squad called Grupo Colina, which formed during the Fujimori administration. Active

Figure 1.1. A classic and iconic image of activist María Elena Moyano on a brick wall in Miraflores that states "María Elena No Está Muerta."

from 1990 to 1994, Grupo Colina targeted university students and other leftist activists in Lima, and impacted the lives of ordinary civilians caught in the conflict.

On July 16, 1992, just months after Moyano's assassination, Sendero Luminoso targeted the upscale Miraflores district with a car bombing that destroyed a residential building and killed more than forty people and injured more than two hundred. Tarata is a side street off a main street called Larco Avenue in a bustling section of Miraflores, and my extended family members heard and felt the bombing in their homes nearby. I remember seeing the pictures of the Tarata bombing in the news, and it took several minutes for my eyes to focus on what exactly I was seeing, which was in essence the obliteration of the front of a building. I could not quite comprehend at that time how a car bombing could inflict so much damage, but I knew that the district would be changed forever—and that the state would predictably mandate an extremely violent response. In April 1992, two years into his presidency and nearly two months after Moyano's assassination, Fujimori initiated the unusual political maneuver of a self-coup. With the country now in upheaval, an attack of Tarata's magnitude seemed imminent. And just three months after the declared self-coup, it became a reality.

Tarata has a very different vibe now. No cars are permitted on the street, creating a surprisingly peaceful walkway off a very bustling Larco Avenue. There is a café, La Paz Cafe (The Peace Café), right next to the site of the bombing, where a water fountain serves as a memorial (see Figure 1.2). The district's elected officials host an annual event in July to commemorate the tragedy. The memorial is a stark reminder that the purpose of the bombing was to instill fear and to terrorize. This street is not near any federal government buildings, which are located in downtown Lima, and surely Sendero Luminoso realized that one of the most effective ways to get the attention of government elites was to attack or terrorize the societal elites, as they often reside in the same district or are even the same people. Even though the street is now closed to car traffic, it feels haunted to me. A 2006 documentary titled *The Fall of Fujimori* contains clips of the bombing's aftermath, as well as news interviews with local residents who are clearly in the throes of trauma, confusion, and rage.[27] One resident being interviewed in the film said, "These sons of bitches need to be killed, exterminated. It's that simple. Even if it sounds extreme to human rights, and the international press." The locals wanted revenge, and so did President Fujimori, who could respond forcefully and without accountability because of the self-coup.

According to Fujimori the self-coup was necessary because of terrorism. However, the Peruvian journalist Philip Mauceri has argued the self-coup was about reshaping and restructuring state power, because by 1992

Figure 1.2. The Tarata memorial in Miraflores commemorating those tragically killed during a bombing by Sendero militants of an apartment building in this location.

there had been a "serious structural deterioration of state power."[28] Mauceri explains that the self-coup could happen because the state's capacity to govern was compromised for several reasons. First, the organization of the state itself was weak. So as the insurgency grew, the state was not in any way prepared to respond to the conflict. Second, the state's influential ability across the country was severely limited. Sendero Luminoso prospered in areas where the state was largely absent. Third, Perú experienced a crisis of international legitimacy when former President García suspended all payment of debt to international banking institutions in the mid-1980s, which ultimately affected Perú's infrastructure and decimated its international standing. In other words, Perú was deeply isolated from other states. If we take all three of these points together, then the crisis in state power was clearly structural. When Fujimori resumed power in 1995, his second term, his goal was in fact to restructure the state so that it could become influential domestically, and so that Perú could improve its standing internationally, particularly among the business community. When Fujimori became president for the first time in 1990, Perú was fragile and ripe for reform. So he set out to "strengthen the state apparatus," especially in parts of the country where the presence of the state did not reach.[29] To establish this state presence, Fujimori began constructing clinics, schools, and other necessary entities in some of the poorest areas of Perú.

Fujimori set out to reconstruct state bureaucracies and structures with less regulation on trade and foreign enterprises, and more privatization, with little regard for labor rights and progressive social policies. The majority of decrees signed by Fujimori during the self-coup period involved neoliberal economic reform and granting new powers to the military. The cornerstone of the reconstruction coalition was the military. The executive decrees were so wide-ranging (some even violated the Constitution at the time) that the Peruvian Congress eventually overturned them. In order to carry out his neoliberal agenda through significant economic reform (which scholars have called Fujishock), Fujimori wanted to strengthen the state to better support capitalism. In other words, the fight against terrorism simultaneously provided the mechanism with which to implement Fujishock.[30]

The passage of the Repentance Law in May 1992, about one month into the self-coup, provided strong incentives to name names of people suspected to be associated with Sendero Luminoso, or who were leftists, with minimal evidence required to convict. This systemic pattern of state abuse continued for many years. When Alan García assumed the presidency for the second time in 2006, he introduced a new law through which human rights cases could be thrown out for dubious reasons. Two presidents from competing political parties shared a common interest in jailing dissidents and perceived rebels as well as downplaying their administration's role in widespread human rights violations during the internal conflict.

The brutality and widespread political corruption continued from 1992–2000. As already stated, 1992 was a difficult year—from continued bombings to an increasing number of disappeared to the self-coup to the eventual capture of Sendero Luminoso's leader Abimael Guzmán. Following Guzmán's capture, the political upheaval continued. By the end of 1992, Fujimori called for the election of a new Congress, now giving him a majority to write a new Peruvian Constitution that would grant him the ability to run for reelection a second time in 2000. He easily won the reelection in

1995 and began to issue presidential pardons of military personnel convicted of human rights abuses, and now he was in a position to run in 2000 for an unprecedented third term due to the change in the Constitution.

The political unrest continued in Fujimori's second term. On December 17, 1996, fourteen Movimiento Revolucionario Túpac Amaru rebels (Revolutionary Movement of Túpac Amaru, MRTA) overtook the Japanese ambassador's residence in Lima and subsequently took hostage a number of prominent Peruvian and Japanese politicians and family members, including Fujimori's mother, which MRTA did not realize at the time.[31] The rebels from this insurgency group eventually released the embassy staff, the women, and the elderly, which included Fujimori's mother. The hostage takeover lasted for 126 days, and on April 22, 1997, Fujimori ordered over one hundred military personnel to raid the residence and violently end the takeover. All fourteen rebels were killed, and video footage released later showed Fujimori inside the residence walking past the dead bodies with pride, as if to send a message about his ruthlessness.

In 2000 Fujimori became embroiled in enormous financial and political scandals, which erupted in September when Vladimiro Montesinos, Fujimori's confidante and intelligence chief, was caught on video bribing politicians from opposing political parties. By November 20, 2000, Fujimori had fled to Japan and faxed in his resignation, and by November 22 Valentín Paniagua (head of Congress) was sworn in as interim president. Elections took place several months later on May 29, 2001, and Alejandro Toledo was then elected the new president of Perú. The 2000s involved the trials and subsequent incarcerations of Montesinos, Fujimori, and a number of others implicated in corruption, scandals, and human rights atrocities during the internal conflict.

Intersectionality and Counterpublic Art Projects

The targeting of public art pieces is an act of extreme right-wing resistance, an exertion of power that is meant to destroy. Decolonial feminist and intersectionality theory can help us understand how this vulgar exertion of power is meant to silence or even retraumatize. This backlash is meant to upend any attempts at memory recovery (see Chapter 2). It also reveals that sectors of the Peruvian dominant public are not simply uninterested in remembering the internal conflict but rather are completely resistant to a version that challenges their complacency, their complicity, and their elitism.

Unlike a museum, to which people make special trips to view art exhibits, these artworks appear in spaces where the public at large can see them, even unexpectedly, as they go about their daily lives. As public artists seek to unsettle and disrupt complacency, provoke dialogue, and compellingly portray aspects of the internal conflict for public consumption, these art projects have been met with resistance by the power of the dominant public that seeks to invalidate, systematically erase, ignore, disregard, reimagine, and/or rewrite the complicated narrative regarding the internal conflict. The dominant public continues to wield a form of power that is political and discursive.

Intersectionality theory advances an understanding of this exertion of power that is "structural and interpersonal."[32] Intersectionality is "an analytical approach for understanding between-category relationships" (race, class, gender, age, sexuality), in which these relationships shape political institutions and social actors, and unsettle the social categories themselves.[33] Since "identity categories of race, gender, and class are shaped by distinct (national) histories and regional contexts," the use of intersectionality must be contextualized.[34] In the context of memory making in postconflict Perú, intersectionality is associated with social location, revealing who has the privilege to not remember and whose voices are silenced. Intersectionality acknowledges the confluence and convergence of identities and social realities that structure sociopolitical hierarchies that reinforce tiers of citizenship.[35]

Intersectionality enhances knowledge about a social issue, problem, or conflict based on the experiences of subordinated groups. The use of an expanded approach to determine what is missing or excluded from an understanding of, in this case, the Peruvian internal conflict, is essential for the construction of memories in the postconflict context. The CVR designated a separate gender program, for example, to directly address the issue of widespread sexual and gender-based violence during the internal conflict.[36] To this end, when "subordinated groups become subjects rather than objects of discourse," they embody the counterpublic sphere.[37] Therefore, the artworks that represent a counterpublic view "challenge and cast doubt" on any mediation of memory works that "selectively manage[s] history in ways that reproduce state hegemony, reinscribing national identity in the fragility after collective violence."[38] The visual representations or themes depicted in the art itself reveal the terrain of power and social location. As Elizabeth Jelin contends, "Identity criteria (ethnicity, race, class, gender) of broadly defined 'victims' become significant in understanding memorialization processes," in part because "historically entrenched cultural domination by other groups result[s] in a lack of autonomous capacity to act in the public sphere."[39]

The two artworks shown in the series of photos in Figures 1.3 and 1.4 seek a deeper engagement with a difficult and conflict-ridden past. A dominant public that is recognized, supported, or emboldened by the state and a counterpublic that seeks to challenge its exclusion are producing conflicting narratives about the internal conflict.[40] Counterpublics, which can be "understood as critical oppositional forces within the society of late capitalism,"[41] are essential to participatory democratic politics. In the case of Perú, the human rights counterpublic aims to rupture a dominant national narrative that absolves the state and the dominant public of their complicity in the violence. The transitional justice art discussed in this chapter is a visual representation of the counterpublic's perspective on the internal conflict and the state's legacies of marginalization.

An intersectionality theoretical approach underscores how the convergence of racism and patriarchy is co-constitutive of realities that should be viewed as interconnected.[42] A feminist approach mandates attention be given to the relationship between power and social location. Its political objective is to recognize communities that have been overlooked or even dismissed and to destabilize fixed social categories of identity (from race/ethnicity to victim/oppressor). This convergence contributes to a far more complicated reality that cannot be contained in a truncated narrative about the internal conflict and its causes as temporally bounded within the two decades of 1980–2000.

Memory production through art is not a linear process because people have different reactions to the work. Some viewers are guided by the heart in relating to the work, but others have a literally violent response, so violent that they attack the symbols that give the art meaning and, by extension, target human rights memory production. The act of attacking public art by attempting to destroy it is a backlash response to advancing a comprehensive understanding about Peruvian history.

Victor Delfín: Human Rights Artist and the APRODEH Mural

When I first arrived at the office of APRODEH, an organization that opened its doors in 1980 at the start of the internal conflict, I was taken aback to see the beautiful mural by Victor Delfín outside its building had been defaced by streaks of black paint (see Figures 1.3a and 1.3b). I had gone to the office in the district of Jesús María in July 2013 to interview Rosario "Charro" Navarez and to arrange a visit to El Ojo Que Llora (APRODEH staff manage access to the memorial site). As I rang the bell to the office building located on a semi-quiet street in Lima, I could not help but feel deeply troubled and disturbed by the ruined mural. The mural had been defaced in response to APRODEH's support for bringing Peruvian president Alberto Fujimori to justice in criminal court for human rights

Figures 1.3a and 1.3b. The mural created by artist Victor Delfín is vandalized with black paint on many parts of the mural outside of the APRODEH building.

violations. Fujimori had fled to Japan in November 2000 but went to Chile in 2005 in an attempt to run in another presidential election. From there he was extradited to Perú and then found guilty of human rights abuses. His supporters, known as Fujimoristas, were angry about the conviction and APRODEH staff widely believed they vandalized the mural as well as El Ojo Que Llora (discussed in the next section).

The mural's creator, Victor Delfín, who is over ninety years old and still creating art, is originally from a small (and now largely abandoned) community called Lobitos in Piura in northwestern Perú. Raised in a poor family, Delfín studied fine arts in Lima in the 1950s. He has earned a reputation for being committed to social justice through his work, and uses a range of mediums for his artistic productions: "wood, metal, canvas, polychrome acrylics and aluminum."[43] One of his massive 1993 sculptures, located in the Parque del Amor (Love Park) in Miraflores, is called *El Beso* (The Kiss). The sculpture shows a couple kissing in a warm and loving embrace. It is a visually stunning piece surrounded by colorful mosaic tiles, affirming love in a city that can sometimes feel heartless.[44]

Delfín is also well known for his embrace of birds and other animals. Christopher B. Condon, director of the Bayard Gallery in New York City, wrote that Delfín does not make sculptures about animals as subjects; instead his sculptures of animals speak of the artist himself, of his Indian and Spanish heritage, and of his own personal mythology, the spirit of which is the archetype that these animals represent.[45] Delfín, along with numerous other artists, stood in strong opposition to Peruvian president Fujimori. The artists denounced Fujimori's self-coup in 1992 and, later, also his daughter, Keiko Fujimori, during her 2011 and 2016 presidential campaigns (presumably Delfín would not have supported her in the 2021 elections either). The artist has also been known to open his home in Barranco, the artist district in Lima, to human rights activist gatherings.

Delfín's mural outside the APRODEH office depicts a genealogy of pain that dates back to the colonial period, but also expresses hope, love, healing, and peace. The top left-hand corner of the mural contains an image of the sun, and the bottom left-hand corner displays excerpts from the articles of the Universal Declaration of Human Rights (UDHR). The portraits of women in different poses (upright and lying in a cradled position) contain a range of emotional expressions (sadness, pain, stoicism). A woman reading a book and a child are situated next to the UDHR image. A cross is located prominently in the center of the mural. The depiction of what appears to be a military officer searching the body of a similarly brown-skinned person to the right as another person looks on appears to be a nod to the surveillance of racialized brown bodies that has become normalized in Perú.

As is common in Delfín's portfolio, birds are depicted prominently in this mural: a condor takes up about a quarter of the space, and is the least damaged; a white bird symbolizing peace at the top right is also untouched. Delfín's affection for and connection to birds in particular not only speaks to "the animals in whose spirit Delfín lives" but is also an acknowledgment of the capacity for human cruelty.[46] For instance, in one of Delfín's earlier paintings depicting a tuberculosis outbreak in a Lima shantytown, text near the bird states, "I renounce humans. I request a bird's passport."

Images of women are on prominent display in this mural. Delfín portrays women outside of a predominantly "victim" imaginary. The images represented in the mural display various forms of power—of legacies of repression of human rights, and of women, children, and the Andean people. The message seems to be about how a colonial legacy and racist patriarchal power have affected people, human rights, and even birds. By depicting women so prominently, Delfín seems to signal a necessary disruption to their marginalization and to suggest that women's energy and presence may be a way forward out of the darkness (note the large image of a woman next to the sun on the left in Figures 1.3a and 1.3b). In addition to acknowledging the relevance of human rights, which is fitting given the organization that commissioned the mural, the artwork also takes us beyond a notion of rights as inherently "human" because of the inclusion of birds and the respect Delfín shows them. Created in October 2001, the APRODEH mural has been damaged at least twice.

Established in 1983, APRODEH is an organization that has been advancing human rights causes since the early years of the internal conflict. The vision statement on its website, which also gets routinely hacked and shut down, reads as follows: "APRODEH hopes that in Peru, human rights inspires ethics transformed by protests, cultural expressions, and inclusive public policies that express all aspects of social, cultural, and political life in a manner in which our rights are equally valid for all."[47] When I asked Rosario why they did not fix the mural again, she cited exhaustion and cost being factors, and that a human rights organization must continue its work undeterred. Moreover, while the destruction of the mural was terrible, its website had been hacked a few weeks before our interview, which had created significant additional problems. She said, "Well, we have lots of cases involving human rights violations, so it's not hard to imagine that they would want to hack it. It's not the first time, but this time we're really struggling to put it back up."

As I kept trying to make sense of why someone would want to destroy such a beautiful mural by a well-known artist, I wondered what the destruction of the mural meant beyond the mere fact of just ruining it. What messages are those who defaced it sending? Given the street location of this mural, violence that would otherwise go unseen now becomes visible to the public. So the targeting of the mural can be interpreted in two ways. First, the use of black paint can represent a blacking out and a violent systematic erasure of the narratives and images conveyed in the mural, a representation of the violence inflicted on Andean citizens in particular, with the streaks resembling a whipping motion. Second, damaging the mural underscores that some people are not ready to confront either the internal conflict or Perú's colonial legacies. The power of art in public spaces, depending on the content and messaging, can awaken individuals out of complacency and routine and make them react rather than reflect.

The mural effectively reflects the hopes and human rights aspirations of those who have been on the margins of dominant power in Perú—for example, women and Andean or Indigenous peoples. There is a spatial distance between those who damaged the mural and those whose bodies and histories are depicted in the work. Whoever destroyed the mural did so out of a visceral reaction to the work of APRODEH on viewing this art. Intentionally damaging artwork is an exertion of "power-over" that stems from a privileged social location, by people who perhaps have never experienced a denial of their human rights or had their humanity questioned. They are part of a dominant public that seeks to silence the memories and counterpublics represented in this mural through their violent act of defacing it.

The mural reflects a painful and complicated history of Peruvian society while conveying an aspirational goal in that the sun, the birds, and human rights will somehow rise and show the way forward. Though the defacement of the mural is a setback and disheartening to view, APRODEH's decision to keep it as is sends an equally powerful message. APRODEH is not trying, for example, to quickly move on and dismiss what has been done to its building, which by extension targets its work. The defaced mural makes visible for all to see the forces APRODEH is up against, and that it will not back down.

According to Delfín, "Nothing is more edifying than going into the streets, joining the clamor of the poor and demanding a more dignified quality of life for my fellow-citizens."[48] Perhaps, then, the mural is making public those demands for dignity and respect. The targeting of the mural is the response to those human rights demands, and yet the demands cannot be ignored. The mural reflects Delfín's own memory of a past as well as a future, similar to what an engagement with decolonial feminism offers us—remembering the past and imagining a future based on transformative memory. Decolonial feminism recognizes that this future emerges from a complicated, not a sanitized, past. Delfín created the mural in the postconflict moment and included colonial precursors in the work itself. The blending of time periods and species is a bridging of the modern (the UDHR) with a fraught legacy of state formation. The attempts to destroy the mural indicate that certain sectors of the dominant public are not receptive to human rights memory by counterpublics. In fact, they want to stop it.

El Ojo Que Llora: "We Are Thinking, We Are Remembering, Our Eyes Crying"

Just like the Delfín mural, the memorial El Ojo Que Llora has been damaged numerous times, with one attack happening in January 2017.[49] Located in the district of Jesús María in Lima, El Ojo Que Llora memorial designed by the late Dutch-born artist Lika Mutal, a longtime resident (for forty-plus years) of Lima, represents tens of thousands of victims of the internal conflict. Numerous events and anniversary commemorations take place at the site. Mutal told US political scientist Katherine Hite that she wished for her memorial to be understood as a humanistic effort to awaken the consciences of all Peruvians to the violence and suffering of the recent past, as well as to encourage reflection regarding the relationships between painful memories and a more just, solidaristic Perú.[50] Mutal, who in 2016 unexpectedly passed away from a stroke at the age of seventy-seven, set out to create a space to memorialize lost lives that could be open to all Peruvians.[51]

Inaugurated on August 28, 2005, El Ojo Que Llora is located off one of the main thoroughfares in the city and borders one of the district's largest public parks, the Campo de Marte (see Figures 1.4a, 1.4b, 1.4c). The memorial's construction took quite some time (to raise funds, select the artist, receive permits, and so forth), and its existence is a testament to activist pressure. Due to routine acts of vandalism committed at the memorial, a security guard is present when the entrance gate is not locked. Yet if people are determined to harm the memorial, they can find a way to do so by jumping the fence.

The centerpiece of the memorial is an enormous stone sitting in a small pond. Mutal found this particular enormous stone on a hill in the northern part of the country, near an ancient cemetery that had been decimated by grave predators. She had the stone brought to her artist studio in Barranco, a coastal artist community in Lima where Delfín also lives. Not being quite

Figures 1.4a, 1.4b, and 1.4c. El Ojo Que Llora with a close-up image of the stones and the centerpiece of the memorial.

sure where it belonged, she had the stone in her studio for several years. She eventually came to realize that it needed to be part of this memorial, with the stone representing Mother Earth (Pachamama). The smaller inserted stone near the top of the larger stone slab is from one of the beaches in Paracas (Ica), also in the northern part of Perú (see Figure 1.4c). This smaller stone is the "eye stone" from which an endless stream of "tears" emanates, representing all of the pain, violence, and grief Mother Earth felt about the internal conflict. Depending on the angle from which one views the centerpiece, it resembles the "three mythical animals of ancient Peruvian civilizations: the peak of the condor, the mouth of a rattlesnake and the silhouette of the puma."[52]

Surrounding the centerpiece are thousands and thousands of stones engraved with the names of the victims of violence. Deciding which names to include on these stones involved its own set of political battles. The original intent was to include the names of all of the victims of violence, including those killed by the state (such as Senderistas, members of the Shining Path). At first, there was really no disagreement about including the names of everyone who had been affected by violence. But soon enough, dissenting voices organized into a formidable campaign against the memorial itself and even renamed it the "Terrorist Memorial." Thus, the memorial has been embroiled in controversy since the beginning, from funding to location to artistic autonomy to what the memorial symbolizes about culpability and victimization. Who is the legitimate victim in this internal conflict? Does the killing of Senderistas merit the same recognition and mourning in this space? These questions came to the fore in November 2006 after the Inter-American Court of Human Rights found the Peruvian government at fault in a raid in May 1992 involving bullets, teargas, and the bombing of the cells in Lima's notorious Miguel Castro Castro Prison, which left forty-one Senderista women dead.[53] With the court declaring the Peruvian government culpable of wrongdoing, the judges stipulated, among other things, that these Senderistas should be part of El Ojo Que Llora. The court ordered economic compensation for the families in addition to having their names added to the memorial site. This fueled the opposition, who placed the fault for the violence solely with Sendero Luminoso and the MRTA (ignoring the fact that the CVR report found the state similarly culpable). The prison raid occurred during the authoritarian rule of President Fujimori. Further, what ultimately led to the uproar regarding the memorial is the fact that the relatives of the Senderistas who were killed at the prison had already arranged for their family members' names to be engraved on the stones.

I was able to see the memorial in 2013 and returned in 2015 to assist APRODEH with the logistics for two events: one in honor of a disappeared husband and father in 2013, and one as part of a school field trip in 2015 (see Chapter 2). When you arrive at the memorial, your eyes go directly to the upright stone in the middle. From the main entrance, you do not notice the small crying eye stone until you walk all the way around to the other side of the sculpture. As detailed by Hite, Mutal demonstrated many layers of thoughtfulness in this design:

> To center her piece, Mutal sculpted a representation of the ancestral goddess Pachamama, Mother Earth. Mutal shaped Pachamama from an ancient, pre-Inca stone she had found on a trek in northern Peru years

before, and in the stone she affixed another rock as an eye. A trickle of water runs continually from the rock, as an eye that cries, that mourns the violence. The stone of Pachamama conveys a maternal quality of the familiarity and ongoing duress of suffering, implicitly against a notion of a masculine inflicting of violence. The representation also projects an eternal sense of victimization, neither periodizing nor romanticizing a "pre-violence" or "pre-conflict" historical moment. Mutal represents the genealogy of the victims as long and deep.[54]

This stone centerpiece sits in the middle of a path shaped like a labyrinth. As you walk this path, stones guide you through the memorial. Many stones are blank, some engravings have been erased by the sun over time, and other engravings are vivid. The stone engravings, done entirely by volunteers, contain the names of the dead and the disappeared. There are also several upright stones in one row of the memorial—these stones are engraved with the names of significant massacres during the internal conflict, such as the Barrios Altos massacre (named for a poor district in Lima where my dad grew up), in which the Fujimori administration ordered a secret military police unit to kill residents suspected of having ties to Sendero Luminoso. This raid included the killing of an eight-year-old boy.

Mutal's artistic decisions reflect a centering of women's energy in response to an exertion of hypermasculine violence. Mutal associates the violence from the internal conflict with the pain inflicted on Mother Earth to such a degree that the earth weeps. In other words, this masculine violence from the internal conflict period is familiar and even felt by Pachamama, by Mother Earth, because Indigenous ancestors have been victims of violence for centuries. Acknowledging the erasures of the histories of violence targeting Indigenous or Andean peoples reveals the entrenched citizenship hierarchies in Perú, based on ethnicity, class, and gender. These erasures rendered Indigenous peoples disproportionately vulnerable to violence during the internal conflict. Thus, this artwork recognizes violence as historical, systemic, and intentional, and renders visible the disproportionate targeting of Indigenous communities.

It is sobering to walk the labyrinth's path and see the thousands of names of unknown people and their years of birth and death—or else just years of birth if they are part of the disappeared. Viewers are left wondering, who is this person? What happened to them? Why did this happen to them? And is this memorial enough? As you walk through the site, pondering unanswerable questions, you eventually make your way to the Pachamama stone. Mutal's design is such that a deceptively modest-sized memorial takes time to walk through; its layout forces you to slow down. The path is designed so that you zigzag through to the end of the memorial and then turn and go back in the direction from which you came. This walking back and forth appears to mirror the nonlinear nature of transitional justice. Just when you think you have made it to the end of a row, you have to make your way back to the other side. After several minutes have passed, you eventually arrive at the centerpiece, the Pachamama stone.

When I first walked along the stone path, I saw that some of the stones had been defaced with orange paint, which had largely faded when I last visited. Repairing the stones can be expensive, and funds are difficult to raise because they have to be privately solicited, since the government will not contribute financially to the memorial. Seeing so many stones ruined, I wondered what someone gains, psychologically or politically, from this kind of destruction. Each stone represents someone's loved one, and ruining the stone is just another form of violence directed at those among the living. During my first trip to the memorial, Rosario told me that stepping on the stones is unacceptable and that visitors must stay on the path the entire time once they have entered the memorial. Stepping on a stone would be like "stepping on the dead," she told me, and the dead have suffered enough.

You can find numerous photos online of the memorial's vandalizations from previous years.[55] In 2007 Mutal asked that there not be a rush to repair the sculpture because it is important to have a frank dialogue about intolerance. In the 2007 incident, the vandals used red paint, which is the color of Fujimori's political party, to damage the memorial. People went to great lengths to damage it, a site known to be meaningful to families and communities that go there in ceremony and for whom it represents a legacy of political violence. Perhaps the people attacking El Ojo Que Llora rationalized their actions because they believed that Fujimori's human rights violations were acceptable. I wonder what kind of "difficult knowledge" they were afraid to learn.

The purpose of El Ojo Que Llora is to provide a space for contemplation, reflection, and grief for disparate communities, a place where demarcations between victim and perpetrator are somewhat blurred. Families and community members whose loved ones are memorialized by the sculpture arrive there seeking comfort and validation. Others, like myself, a member of a transnational family connected to Perú, are forced to contemplate complicity and the enormity of the tragedy. Mutal's reasoning for excluding Senderistas as legitimate victims of the violence, as not "deserving victim status," despite the Inter-American Court's controversial decision mentioned above, contradicts her stated intent of a "solidaristic Perú." This view reinscribes a stifling binary of "victim" and "perpetrator" that does not align with the work of scholars of Peruvian history.[56]

Given the controversies exposed by the court's decision, deciphering who embodies "deserving victim" status for inclusion in the memorial becomes critical to challenge. Paulo Drinot asks, "Under what circumstances could victimizers be victims?" He connects the naming of victims to the interpretation of violence, specifically the perpetrators of violence.[57] Further, as Margarita Saona points out, this remembrance of the victims of violence, particularly when their names are displayed, gets tangled in the memory battles about innocence and responsibility. Those who have studied the communities who have suffered the most in the internal conflict know that categorizing victims and perpetrators is a complex issue.[58] As Katherine Hite states, "Victims, perpetrators, resisters, and survivors come from many sides of the conflict and can often be read as all of the above and more."[59] In the case of the categories delineated by Hite—victim, perpetrator, resister, and survivor—one person can occupy one or more of these categories simultaneously. To understand why in one instance an Andean villager is an innocent victim and in another context a perpetrator, one has to consider the circumstances and social conditions in which those categories are utilized and to what benefit.

After the terrorist attacks in the United States on September 11, 2001, transnational feminist scholars urged a recognition of "the gendered and ethnocentric history of sentimentality, grief, and melancholy that have been mobilized."[60] This same perspective can apply to transitional justice in Perú given the reaction to the creation of this particular memorial and the debates regarding who is deserving of victim status in the aftermath and who merits grief. Feminist intersectionality theory challenges fixed categories and identities, in particular because, as Elizabeth Jelin argues, "identities have to be conceived as historical constructs, with blurred and changing boundaries" because "no community will be homogenous."[61] Thus, neither the victims nor the perpetrators should be homogenized, because reifying a deserving victim status will result in the impossible task of identifying innocence that is in tension with complex subjectivity.

This tense and awkward, but necessary, convergence of people affected by state and terrorist violence and those on the margins of that violence becomes possible through this memorial. Those who stand against what the memorial represents are members of a dominant public that is unwilling or unprepared to process the internal conflict in a way that is fundamentally healing. As Saona states, "A monument conceived as a symbol for peace revealed how truth and reconciliation are not achieved by decree. The names on the stones bring together the innocent ones and the ones who were agents of violence, and this, in fact, might lead its visitors to reexamine the past."[62] I would also argue that in this reexamination, this kind of framing of the stones—"innocent ones" and the "agents of violence"—should be upended as well because the criteria for determining the status of innocent and perpetrator belie the realities of the internal conflict itself.

One of the core tensions El Ojo Que Llora raises collectively is around who merits mourning and who does not. The backlash directed at the memorial is not merely a disagreement over this core tension but rather a refusal to even have the discussion. A critical human rights memory is not invested in delineating a clear divide between deserving and undeserving victim, even though the politics of El Ojo Que Llora became mired in that controversy. Rather, a critical human rights memory recognizes that a collective harm and trauma has been released, and it requires as honest an assessment as possible about the roots of that harm and trauma. El Ojo Que Llora represents this recognition by asking visitors to pause, reflect, and remember. It becomes less relevant where to direct our grief, and more to acknowledge this process as part of our journey to reach transformative memory. El Ojo Que Llora conveys that the internal conflict must never be repeated, and in order for that to be viable, we must collectively grieve and honor the dead.

Conclusion

After an incredibly fraught two decades of internal conflict, Perú arrived uneasily at a postconflict period after 2000. Art provided an outlet to engage this new time period. In postconflict Perú, art depicting some aspect of the internal conflict is meant to offer a critique or layered commentary on what happened, as well as provide a moment of pause to contemplate the breadth, depth, and extent of the violence. These dissident artistic engagements occur within a context in which the powerful and elite from the dominant public converge to stymie representations by the counterpublic. As Cynthia Milton argues in the case of Perú, "Art offers a powerful means for recounting the past and for reaching a kind of understanding."[63] So how do we reach that understanding and then go beyond it? And how can we engage with intersectionality, which is illustrative for acknowledging the differential experiences with violence and trauma in the journey to reaching this new understanding?

Delfín's mural on APRODEH's building depicts respect for human rights and the legacy effects of repressive rule dating back to the colonial period. The mural's destruction by streaks of black paint indicates that the road to healing and peace remains long. The controversies surrounding the inclusion of Senderista victims in El Ojo Que Llora because they did not meet some arbitrary criteria of "deserving victim" status in the court of the dominant public's opinion reify a narrow construction of "victim" that elides complex subjectivity.

The defacing of the APRODEH mural and El Ojo Que Llora is a reminder that human rights art is provocative, especially in Perú, where open hostility to human rights is strong. The backlash responses indicate that deep-seated racism has led to a fragmented society, and that it is extremely difficult to repair or restore society when too many are undisturbed by someone else's pain. And yet, the very reasons why the artworks are attacked remind us of their importance. Efforts to memorialize the internal conflict through art, or to delegitimize those artistic endeavors through acts of violence are about the stakes involved in representing the internal conflict period beyond a state-dominated or state-absolving narrative. By focusing on art that is accessible to the public and that represents a counterpublic point of view, these art projects are part of a democratic project of inclusivity, visibility, and accountability. The hostile reaction to memory projects undergirds some of the longstanding resentment of and anger about what these artworks represent and are trying to commemorate. What is most troubling is how the attacks on these works of art are also attacks on the artists and their visions—in terms of their hopes as well as their contribution to reconciliation and healing.

These public art projects are also about the building of human rights memory that is ultimately culturally transformative following an incredibly violent and traumatizing internal conflict. This transformation requires an engagement with the trajectory of political violence from the colonial period through the internal conflict and thus relies on the formation of memories that are comprehensive and that implicate complicit elites. The backlash to human rights memory should not be dismissed as the actions of merely "bad individuals" engaged in acts of violence. Their actions occur within a cultural context that normalizes this kind of display of violence. The attacks on these public art projects occurred at a time when perpetrators—in this case Fujimori and his enablers—were being held accountable through the legal process and system. So outraged were the Fujimoristas by this overdue accountability that they attacked public art projects—including the one that was explicitly designed with the intention of bringing directly and indirectly affected communities together in reflection and dialogue. With the suppression of memory comes silence. Therefore, achieving transformative memory requires a counterprocess of memory recovery, the subject of the next chapter.

For the Delfín mural, the process of transformative memory must acknowledge the Spanish conquest. This is a critical point of departure in a Eurocentric society such as Perú as it directly challenges the anti-Indigenous racism that has informed the social and citizenship hierarchies that denigrate anyone Indigenous. For El Ojo Que Llora, the transformative memory is about a difficult time in which the artist Mutal imagines or hopes for a solidaristic postconflict Perú. Acknowledging Pachamama is perhaps a way to engage in this remembering that will indeed be transformative. Mutal's work asks its human viewers to remember our relationship to Mother Earth, as this is a connection we all share.

The backlash to human rights memory clarifies how challenging it will be to achieve a "solidaristic Perú." A backlash can feel like a setback. But viewing it only as a setback misses the mark too. Backlashes, once we pick ourselves back up again, can be moments to repair the community. Engaging new constituencies can make human rights memory more powerful. Can the backlash produce different conversations with new constituencies about why the provocation even occurred (of attacking the public art)? Can the backlash produce a set of conditions in which memory recovery—a process of asking people to openly discuss the internal conflict in order to awaken their suppressed memories—unfold? The next chapter explores these questions by underscoring that reaching transformative memory is possible once memories have been recovered through dialogue, reflection, and empathy.

CHAPTER 2

Memory Recovery through Art and Education

A Latin American artist cannot remain indifferent to the reality of violence, hunger, misery, abuse and corruption surrounding us.
—Peruvian artist Victor Delfín, *Delfín*

In August 2015, I ran into Kristell, a Peruvian friend I had met the previous year at a conference in Durham, North Carolina. On this day, we were attending an arts and social change conference in Lima. We had hit it off right away when we met in North Carolina but had lost touch once the conference concluded. Now we stared at each other for a bit, almost in disbelief that we would randomly run into each other in Lima after so many months. After realizing that we were not figments of each other's imagination, we exchanged hugs and kisses and did a quick catch-up before the conference started up again after the break. We said our goodbyes at the conclusion of the conference and promised to meet up again before I left Lima. I emailed her a few days later to ask if she wanted to go see the renowned theater group Yuyachkani perform *Sin Titulo*, which had debuted in 2003. I knew the play was about the internal conflict, but I didn't really know much more than that. I knew this would be of interest to her based on our conversations. She too had been wanting to see the play for some time and was more than happy to join me.

We met up near the Miraflores apartment I was renting, and took a couple of microbuses to the theater in a different district. As we sat in the theater's café having tea, we started to talk about why we wanted to see this play and our excitement about finally being able to do so. Kristell is from the postmemory generation, and did not directly experience the devastation of the internal conflict given her young age in 2000, but she had quite a bit of knowledge and some critical analysis that she had learned in her university studies and from her family. She talked about the internal conflict and her memories in a way that made it clear she questioned the narrative of the state being the "savior of the nation."

Sin Titulo has been described as "a great installation-stage action on the borders of document theater, visual arts and performance, where actors and spectators share the same space, which suggests the attic of a history museum where documentation, images and elements from two periods of Peruvian history converge, the Pacific War (19th century) and the internal armed conflict (20th century)."[1] Seeing the play was a very powerful experience. As it was about to start, we were moved into a long rectangular-shaped room where we could peruse tons of old magazines, newspapers, display cases, video clips, and so forth. The space got quite crowded, and Kristell and I found each other every few minutes as we wandered about checking out the material. Most of it had to do with the internal conflict, as if to take the entire audience back to that time period. From there, we were escorted into a dark room next door. As we whispered to each other, "I wonder what's next," the play began. The stage platforms moved throughout the room; the audience was in no way a passive observer. I was not accustomed to walking around so much during a performance! The connections the artists made between the Pacific War and the internal conflict was not a disjointed narrative. By linking these two critical points of Peruvian history as bookends, *Sin Titulo* as a theatrical performance conveyed how the temporality of the internal conflict as captured by the Comisión de la Verdad y Reconciliación (CVR) report was an incomplete portrait; the memory of the internal conflict should not be fragmented.

Artistic memory productions serve as necessary reminders for the public audience, in which the performers engage in and embody acts of remembrance. A performance like this one stays with you long after its conclusion. As one interprets the art, one's positionality also enters the space. In other words, I am viewing it as someone from the diaspora, Kristell is viewing it as someone from the postmemory generation, and others in the audience are viewing it as closely connected to their lived experiences. And so in all three of these groupings, memories have to be recovered. The recovery will eventually lead to the restoration of fragmented ties, but as discussed in Chapter 1, the backlash remains ever lurking.

This chapter examines the recovery of human rights memories through art and community education projects.[2] This method of recovering memory is a journey that is neither linear nor every truly complete. The journey has some detours because these societal transitions do not occur outside of a sociopolitical national or global context, nor in a vacuum. This chapter discusses two human rights art projects, a revisit to El Ojo Que Llora memorial and a traveling museum called Museo Itinerante Arte por la

Memoria, as well as a human rights education project, El Reloj de Memoria (The Memory Clock), developed by the Instituto Peruano de Educacíon en Derechos Humanos y la Paz (The Peruvian Institute of Education in Human Rights and Peace). These projects share a common and complementary goal for memory recovery. My discussion of El Ojo Que Llora in this chapter is about a commemoration event for Javier, who became a disappeared person in 1994. Commemoration events occur every month at the memorial, which has been vandalized at least eight times, according to La Coordinadora Nacional de Derechos Humanos.[3]

This chapter explores how art and community education projects addressing the internal conflict are contributing to a democratic representation of truth telling by asking us to do the difficult work of reflection and recovery in order to chart a different future. At a time when sociopolitical unrest is the norm in Perú and other parts of the world, it can be difficult to make intentional space for memory recovery. Memories for memories' sake is not the point. Transformative memory is about a willingness and intention to embark on a new future with courage, which is essential for any genuine social and cultural change.

In general, memory studies "holds positive connotations, despite the negative memories themselves."[4] Further, as Cynthia Milton asks, "What about 'memories' that script a present and future based on a distorted past?"[5] Here she is referencing the memories of armed state agents, which she calls "conflicted memory." Not all of the agents engaged in indiscriminate repression, as she was reminded by audience members during research talks in Lima. But that doesn't absolve the violent actions ordered by the state. Hence, memory recovery can reveal that an individual's memory may come into tension with what happened on a larger scale. There is also a presumption here that if we remember truthfully, we will not repeat mistakes. If only it were that simple.

The website Facing History provides educators with a model for engaging with contentious topics. It notes that meaningful learning happens for students when the intellectual is coupled with "emotional engagement" and "ethical reflections" in order to understand why certain tragic and contentious events occurred in society; it categorizes this convergence as the "pedagogical triangle." The website states, "This integration of head, heart, and ethics is always important to learning, and it's particularly crucial when students are considering contentious and troubling news."[6] This pedagogical triangle is a useful framework and arguably necessary for reaching transformative memory. Importantly, though, there must be an openness to learning and a space to do so in order to engage mind, heart, and ethics when seeking to reflect and rebuild society when it has been broken. All three art projects discussed in this chapter engage in this triadic convergence of heart, mind, and ethics in ways that complement one another. I begin the next section with El Ojo Que Llora, a space meant to foster deep reflection—again, to engage heart, mind, and ethics simultaneously—in order to recover memory. Even though the memorial has been attacked, it remains a critical space for public grieving, community-centered memory recovery, and honoring the dead and disappeared.

El Ojo Que Llora: A Space for Grieving and Memory Recovery

Peruvian and controversial author Mario Vargas Llosa refers to El Ojo Que Llora as "the paradox that is art and life" wherein "horror and suffering" could be "capable of generating . . . something so intense and so beautiful."[7] The paradox underscores the importance of political art in provoking dialogue and debate and, at least in one case, exposing pain. Peruvian society has to be ready for that provocation and resist the tendency to think of acknowledging pain as being on a linear road to healing.

I helped APRODEH with a family event to honor a disappeared person named Javier at El Ojo Que Llora. Javier and his wife Sonia had been very politically active, particularly in labor union movements. At the time of his disappearance in 1989, their two daughters were three and six years old. The younger daughter has no memories of her father, but the older one does (in her late twenties at the time of this commemoration event, she remains quite traumatized by what happened to her father). When it became evident to Sonia that something terrible had happened to Javier, she knew that they had to flee. They fled to Bolivia in 1989 or 1990. They lived there for over two decades, fearful to return to Lima because of the death threats Sonia and her young family had received and because others they had known and loved had also disappeared. In April or May 2012, they returned to Lima for the first time since they began living in exile. One of the first things Sonia wanted to do when she returned to Lima was to organize a commemoration of Javier's life, because for the past two decades her family and their broader community of support had never been able to grieve, never been able to come together, and had instead been kept in emotional suspense.[8]

The ceremony was well attended and touching. Dozens of community members, activist comrades, and family members came to the site. They brought flowers and other items such as candles. The group initially gathered under a tent so that a few people could first address the crowd, including Sonia, and then the group walked in procession on the gravel walkway to Javier's stone, which was surrounded by candles and flowers. One of my roles was to make sure that people remained on the gravel path and that no one stepped on the other stones. After additional words were spoken at Javier's stone (at this point I was standing at a distance out of respect for those who had gathered), they regrouped under the tent for a reception.

These gatherings happen in spite of the city's efforts to derail them. A city permit is needed for a gathering to take place at El Ojo Que Llora, especially because microphones and loudspeakers are required. During the gathering for Javier, the local district also issued a city permit for a very loud music concert across the street but conveniently forgot to turn on the electricity for Javier's gathering. This made it nearly impossible to hear the speakers, including Javier's wife, especially if one was standing at the back of the large group. Apparently, when it comes to events at the memorial it is common practice for district employees to find ways to undermine the gathering in any way possible. But people who are ready to honor someone they love are not deterred by the actions of the local district office.

This experience led me to realize the importance of having a public space to grieve, process and reflect, and even celebrate in community. A rupture in the deafening silence regarding the devastation of the internal conflict occurs when communities grieve and gather for all to see. The ritual and spiritual dynamic of coming together in this public space, at this public memorial, produces a collective or community-wide grieving moment. One has to process what happened in order to imagine something new. In other words, processing a long overdue heartache needed to happen before Sonia, her daughters, and the extended family and community could even think about building a different life than the one they had imagined before Javier became one of the disappeared. El Ojo Que Llora provides a vital public space that acknowledges the devastation of the violence that has touched so many lives.

For the ceremony, candles had been lit throughout the memorial, including a candle next to a stone engraved with Javier's name; the wind eventually blew out every single candle at the site except for the one next to his stone. Rosario "Charro" Navarez of APRODEH, who had arranged my visit, whispered to me how incredible it was that the candle remained lit. "Javier must be here in some way," she said. As I reflect on that pivotal moment about the candle remaining lit, I do not want to dismiss that moment as random; the spiritual is powerful, after all. Drawing from feminist scholars who challenge the privileging of secularism in research, such as Gloria Anzaldúa, Leela Fernandes, and Maria Lugones, this "research moment" reminded me of a haunting quote by M. Jacqui

Alexander: "The dead do not like to be forgotten, especially those whose lives had come to a violent end."[9]

Alexander also reminds us of the importance of the sacred for "transnational feminism and related research projects, beyond an institutionalized use value of theorizing marginalization."[10] Alexander's point is well taken; when I visited the memorial site in 2013, it was difficult to deny the sacredness of the space. Should I consider the burning candle Javier's way of communicating with us, of helping those gathered in their memory recovery? If so, what was Javier trying to tell the people who gathered there for him? Anzaldúa's work also intimately ties spirituality with knowledge production, challenging modernist ontologies that not only separate spirituality from knowledge production but also devalue it. Further, as Maria Lugones contends, spirituality, or the spirit world, is central to the praxis of decolonial feminism in that women of color are "the fractured locus," and thus, from this location, "important epistemological shift[s]" occur.[11] The fractured locus does not have to apply exclusively to women of color, per se; therefore, what can we learn from the fractured locus of the disappeared, from those who were targets of state-sanctioned violence and of the terrorist groups?

As I witnessed in this family dynamic, anger, confusion, and resentment remain. Whatever dreams Sonia and Jorge had for their family vanished overnight, and there is real generational sadness as a result. Moreover, can we accept that anger, confusion, and resentment may exist for those who targeted Jorge as well, albeit for different reasons? In other words, is there a space in which to increase the capacity for bereaving and for recovering memories from that grief? Since there is no singular memory, how can El Ojo Que Llora enable a multitude of memories to emerge? If we're seeking transformative memory, then El Ojo Que Llora is not selective about whom Pachamama is weeping for; the tears are for everyone.

The Memory Game: Human Rights Popular Education and Curriculum

Created by the Instituto Peruano de Educación en Derechos Humanos y la Paz, the game El Reloj de Memoria (The Memory Clock) is played in groups with a maximum of six people. Each group takes cards with different colors. Each card contains a key action or word in four categories: Recordando (Remembering), Reflexionando (Reflecting), Recomendando (Recommending), and Recreándonos (Recreating). As Pablo Zavala of the Instituto Peruano shared with me during our interview, the purpose of the education game is to get participants to engage with their memories or draw out their knowledge about the internal conflict for a group discussion.

As the players take turns, someone is supposed to move the clock handle and land on a color. When they arrive at a color they need to remain on that card's subject for about two minutes. Each color has six cards designated to it. The game concludes when all of the cards have been reviewed and discussed. The game also suggests a ten-minute debrief to respond to the following questions:

- How did you feel about the game?
- Who do you think this game is meant for?
- What conclusions did we arrive at by the end of the game?

After discussing these debriefing questions and others that may have come up in conversation, the game concludes. Pablo shared that they took this game throughout the country to create openings in which to discuss the internal conflict within communities differently affected by the conflict. At first sight, the colors and cartoon caricatures on the cards and game board hide the serious nature of the game. And yet within a few minutes it is clear that difficult subjects are being broached here.

This section begins by reviewing the questions, statements, and tasks that correspond to each of the four aforementioned categories. There is no defined order to reacting or responding to any of the statements or questions detailed on the cards. Then we examine how each part of the game creates space for learning, engagement, and transformation. The game provides an entry point or road map to navigating the politics of memory recovery and proceeds in a manner that is intentionally challenging yet hopeful and forgiving. It offers a community-based approach to holistic human rights education in which all parts of the game complement each other. For this discussion, we begin with the key actions of Remembering, Reflecting, Recommending, and Recreating. Remembering acknowledges the participants' starting point, and Reflecting asks them to actively retrieve their memories. Recommending and Recreating build from the foundation of Remembering and Reflecting. The intention of Recommending is to devise a plan of action. And Recreating specifically asks participants to chart out their ideas for a just and equitable future.

Remembering and Reflecting: The Foundation of Human Rights Memory

For every section of the Memory Game, each participant is invited to respond to the various prompts. The Remembering prompts (Table 2.1) are an example of what scholars of pedagogy consider "retrieval." With Remembering, the participants are asked to remember the conflict—to

Table 2.1. List of questions and prompts pertaining to the "Remembering" section of the game

REMEMBERING
• Talk about an individual or collective response to violence. • Offer a fact about violence caused by the Shining Path and the armed forces. • Do you know how the villagers reacted to the incursion of the armed forces? • Do you remember someone who was considered a hero or a shero? • Share with the group a situation in which you were scared during those years of violence. • Have your parents or grandparents talked about what happened in previous years? • Talk about an event or fact of violence that brought consequences to your community. • Share if you had a family member or friend who was a victim of violence.

literally recover that memory from their consciousness and share it with the group. The Remembering theme includes addressing how a participant may have been personally affected and situates the violence by asking the group to reflect on how others in their nearby communities or families reacted or responded to the violence. The items related to fear, victim status, and generational knowledge offer insights into the different elements of memory recovery associated with this particular internal conflict.

From these prompts, the issue of violence is addressed from multiple vantage points: from that of the individual, the collective, the parents and grandparents, a friend, and the community. The Memory Game asks participants to address their fears during this time as well as to acknowledge someone who perhaps did something courageous. A couple of the prompts also ask participants to disclose violent events that harmed the community as well as to identify victims in their families or communities. Retrieving these incidents from one's memory can be very challenging given the natural tendency to suppress trauma. And yet remembering can be especially critical in shaping the public narrative about memory during the two decades of internal conflict that began in 1980. At the same time, the questions go beyond the official years of the internal conflict. Four of the points from Remembering are declarative statements, encouraging the group to share responses to violence (events or other facts) and to talk about victims of violence. If engaged effectively, the discussion prompts could illuminate a path to memory recovery.

From Remembering comes Reflecting, for which a new set of cards offers questions associated with violence as well (Table 2.2). As with the Remembering prompts, the discussion of violence is not limited to the internal conflict period. It asks the group to think about corporal punishment in the

Table 2.2. List of questions and prompts pertaining to the "Reflecting" section of the game

REFLECTING
• Why do you think that the Shining Path in Perú emerged? • What should we do so that the history of violence does not repeat? • Do you think that violence solves the problems of the country? • What do you think has generated violence in Perú? • Who was most affected by the internal armed conflict in Perú? • Do you think there is a connection between violence and the use of punishment at school? • Why do you think the armed forces responded in such a violent manner during the internal conflict? • Why do you think Peruvians ask government leaders to rule with an iron fist?

schools, to reflect on those most affected by violence, and even to reckon with perpetual violence. Of particular note is the question about why many Peruvians supported authoritarian rule following Alberto Fujimori's regime. As mentioned before, Fujimori's own daughter, Keiko Fujimori, has come extremely close to winning the presidency multiple times (in 2011, 2016, and 2021).[12] As a member of Fuerza Popular, her father's political party, Keiko would likely run the country in the same manner as her father did. As voting in Perú is mandatory, the fact that she loses by a razor-thin margin every time is an indication of the fraught political situation in the conflict's aftermath.

For the Reflecting questions, participants are encouraged to speak candidly about their thoughts on the emergence of the Shining Path, colonial violence, and state-sanctioned terror and to link their thoughts to the authoritarian impulse prevalent in Peruvian culture. Acknowledging the unstable footing of democratic rule in Perú that preceded the internal conflict,[13] this set of questions assesses participants' knowledge of violence in Perú in a nonjudgmental way. The question-and-answer format is a valuable way to get people to ponder and interrogate their own taken-for-granted assumptions about why the conflict emerged without situating any of the participants as more knowledgeable than the others.

The Remembering questions lead participants to a process of conjuring up memories, some of which may have been suppressed. As those memories are retrieved, it becomes possible to reflect on those memories. As memories are released and shared in the space of community, an opportunity presents itself to then revisit and reremember, or to learn of other participants' memories in the game. Remembering and Reflecting form a critical foundation on which to build upon the remaining two parts of the game: Recommending and Recreating. Memory production must have a purpose and an intention in order to result in a transformative memory that builds on or is linked to decolonial feminism, especially since the specter of Spanish colonization looms large.

Recommending and Recreating: Coimagining a Different Perú

With the foundation of the game established, the remaining two game categories—Recommending and Recreating—are about charting a different course and future for the country. Recommending (Table 2.3) asks for concrete next steps, a plan of action. These steps are for thinking about not only the most vulnerable communities but also larger democratic visions. As for Recreating, these statements are trying to bring communities torn apart back together—literally or metaphorically. This final set of game prompts, as discussed below, are somewhat joyful.

The Recommending prompts ask participants to think about ways to redefine the meaning and purpose of multicultural education, of promoting literacy, of eliminating educational disparities in rural education, and of having violence-free schools. The eight prompts could be considered the beginning of a recommendations plan of transitional justice with regard

Table 2.3. List of questions and prompts pertaining to the "Recommending" section of the game

RECOMMENDING
• Establish a curriculum that stimulates and guides knowledge toward well-being in order to achieve comprehensive training and a distance from the proclivity for violence; a reformulation of simplistic and distorted visions of Peruvian history and reality.
• Give urgent attention to the most vulnerable population: start with the smallest in the neediest areas.
• Strengthen instances of participation and democratization of schools.
• Prohibit the use of any form of physical punishment or humiliating practices as a form of disciplining and an exertion of violence.
• Redefine education in terms of content, methodologies, and topics covered based on access to the labor market, placing emphasis on the rural population. Restore dignity to and increase quality of rural schools.
• Promote respect to ethnic and cultural differences in education. Adapt the school in all its aspects to the ethnic-linguistic, cultural, and geographical diversity of the country.
• Emphasize educational policies aimed at the transformation of the school such that the human condition of the students is respected and contributes to the integral development of their personality. Achieve an awareness of peace and affirm education as its instrument.
• Promote a literacy plan with priority given to adolescent and adult women in rural areas.

to education—a plan that asks for not only policy reform but also community development, social reform, and social justice. The Recommending prompts delve directly into the tiers of citizenship that have remained intact for generations as so many parts of the country have been forgotten.

The Recommending prompts can be described as a two-pronged approach to education, focusing on both the curriculum and the democratization of schooling. The Recommending section clearly identify that a critical intervention is needed within the school setting, especially in rural parts of the country. According to Statista, as of 2017, only 28 percent of rural residents achieve a high school education, leaving an overwhelming majority never acquiring more advanced literacy, linguistic, and math skills.[14] Reaching a certain educational level does not signify that students have obtained a quality education, though, nor that the curriculum respects the linguistic and cultural diversity of the country.

The focus on education, starting at the primary level, reveals the transformative potential of knowledge, cross-cultural understanding, and history. The memories of violence cannot be disassociated from how the state has completely abandoned rural parts of the country by not investing in these areas. The abandoned citizenry have futures destined for trauma and hardship unless serious financial and political investments take place to provide quality education and infrastructure.

The final part of the game uses the Recreating statements (Table 2.4) to establish a level of warmth, community, and camaraderie among the participants. What is compelling about these statements is the affect dimension. From creating a personalized greeting to hugging the person next to you to forming a timeline based on birth years, Recreating is about establishing and solidifying connections. It is about rupturing the tiers of citizenship that contributed to the longevity and brutality of the internal armed conflict.

The song "Flor de Retama," composed by Ricardo Dolorier from Ayacucho, tells of the uprising that occurred in the region on June 22, 1969, when the military government of Juan Velasco Alvarado proposed to do away with offering free education if students failed their subjects. The uprising resulted in police killing local residents, including students. This song, as opposed to the national anthem, is one pertinent to Recreating, to rebuilding a fractured society. Dolorier considers the song to be a recounting of a tragedy as well as a protest. Rosmery Anni Barrientos Castañeda recounts:

> These events (in Huanta) took place during the military government of Juan Velasco Alvarado [when his administration issued] Decree Law No. 006, aimed at charging for free education in secondary education; that

Table 2.4. List of questions and prompts pertaining to the "Recreating" section of the game

RECREATING
• Invent a form of greeting and share it with your group. • Give a hug to your partner on the left and wish them something (positive) for their future. • Make a proclamation for peace. • Find a partner from another group and dedicate a poem about the importance of Indians ("cholos") in the country. • Make a timeline using your birth dates. • Sing and comment on the song "Flor de Retama." • Create and adapt a song that promotes the eradication of discrimination.

is, if the students failed in any subject, they were required to pay 100 soles per month . . . . However, the decree law was rejected by parents, peasants and students throughout the country, to which [Humanities scholar] Vich . . . stated: "It was in Huanta where the largest and bloodiest protest took place. The main newspapers assured that ten thousand peasants took the city and that the mob attacked the police posts with an uncontainable fury. The confrontation resulted in around 50 dead and 37 arrested." After this event, Ricardo Dolorier Urbano was inspired to create this musical composition.[15]

Other artists drew similar inspiration, as Ayachucan artist Edilberto Jiménez created a *retablo* (Peruvian folk art that is contained in a box) of the same name.[16]

Any form of recreating must underscore that the infrastructures in place, or lack thereof, have failed people. The view that certain citizens were not worthy of any education, as access to schooling would render them upwardly mobile subjects, is a relic of coloniality. Thus, if colonial patriarchy entrenched the citizenship hierarchy, decolonial feminism will undo it. The Recreating statements are advancing a decolonial feminist approach through their emphasis on creativity and connection—from greetings to hugs to songs. Colonialism was meant to divide us, so decoloniality is about restoration.

The Memory Game encourages participants to develop a human rights vision for the future. Recovering memory or openly speaking about this difficult period is not an easy undertaking, because everyone has to arrive at the game with an openness to listening and to being heard and even with a willingness to admit one may not have responses to all of the queries. This creative education project delves into a difficult and complicated topic in a gentle way. As the pedagogical triangle from Facing History reveals, heart, intellect, and ethics must come together in order for meaningful or deep learning to occur. This game accomplishes this merger in every set of prompts. Memories regarding the internal conflict cannot stay at the level of the intellectual, of the mind; nor can they remain at the level of the heart, which could result in a paternalistic empathy. The dimension of ethics leads us to identify a set of values, of principles, that must be shaped by the heart and mind. From this convergence, decolonial feminism can then provide a path forward.

Museo Itinerante Arte por la Memoria and the Preservation of Memory Everywhere

A counterpublic group of artists committed to promoting dialogue and memory retrieval and reflection everywhere launched Museo Itinerante Arte por la Memoria.[17] In the summer of 2013 I came to engage with some of these artists, who identify themselves as human rights, public, and political artists. They create murals, sculptures, and paintings and perform plays. They use the internet to showcase their work and organize art showings at community centers, and they have also held exhibits in the open plazas of downtown Lima and throughout Perú. Museo Itinerante has become a point of departure for other artistic projects as well, such as community murals. Artists from this same group also created a separate project called Lugar de la Memoria (Place of Memory), in which they mark a site with a sign to inform the public that human rights violations occurred there. Their intent is to use art to raise awareness, provoke discussion, and enact social justice as part of their contribution to transitional justice efforts.

Jorge is a human rights artist of Japanese-Peruvian descent. During our interview, he stressed that art is what will lead to the cultural transformation needed in Perú because art affects people. He said, "The most radical change, the deepest change, should be cultural," and he believes that art is the ideal vehicle for this cultural transformation. We spoke about some of his art displays in Perú, including one he created with an artist friend, Mauricio, in Villa El Salvador. Formed in 1973, Villa El Salvador is a poor and working-class municipality district (considered a shantytown because of the lack of water and electricity) based in the southern outskirts of Lima where residents engage in the practice of self-governance. Villa El Salvador is the community where Senderistas assassinated Afro-Peruvian social activist María Elena Moyano on February 15, 1992, as mentioned in Chapter 1.[18]

Museo Itinerante Arte por la Memoria is a traveling museum comprised of artworks that condemn complicity from those in government leadership positions and those who simply looked the other way. This group of artists felt compelled to get organized during a 2009 event commemorating Fujimori's self-coup. Their first project was "a street exhibit just with artworks that denounced the crimes of Fujimorismo."[19] Part of what these artists are doing in their work is debating memory—who remembers what, and from whose perspective, whose memories get validated, and which ones get disregarded. In 2009, some seventeen years after Fujimori's self-coup, these activists wanted to commemorate this anniversary through an artistic intervention. Jorge explained:

> To our surprise, [the street exhibit] was a success. People debated right there, they fought, they commented. And when we analyzed it, we realized that art had a strong potential to deal with human rights issues, and we said "why don't we formalize this project and do traveling exhibits in different places, in public spaces, talking about human rights?" And that's how the idea for the itinerant museum, "art for the memory," came about, taking an art exhibit that deals with human rights violations or with the history of political violence in this country to different parts of the country.

This experience proved transformative for the artists; they realized the importance of engaging the public, of engaging people with whom they would not normally interact in their social and political circles. Fierce public debates, such as the one spurred by this street exhibit, may be interpreted as rude or disrespectful in the United States, but in Perú these exchanges are not viewed in the same way. As the artists debriefed about the experience, the strong potential of art to address human rights issues became crystallized.

Jorge and his artist colleagues have also participated in community-based workshops on mural making. On one occasion, the artists associated with the itinerant museum received a request to travel to Pampachacra, a rural community in Ayacucho that had experienced a disproportionately high level of violence during the internal conflict. The Pampachacra community had built a communal site as a place of memory using the modest reparation money they received from the government, and now they wanted to add a mural. Here's how Jorge described this mural-making experience:

> They asked us to go and paint a mural there [in Pampachacra]. We have always rejected the idea that artists are illuminated beings that show up

with an idea and others have to accept it. To us, everything that is done for the people, without the people, is against the people. We did a workshop with them. We did a workshop to see what they wanted to paint, and we painted the murals with them. To our surprise, they didn't want one mural but three. One was of the community before the violence, another one during the violence, and another one after the violence. And it's very interesting that the last mural shows the community having a party and it says, "we won" ("*triunfamos*"). So sometimes one can have an urban, middle-class outlook and think that it's a poor community, one with lots of needs, but they see themselves as winners because they won against political violence. They won against unfavorable conditions, when all the odds were against them.

Jorge's description of the mural-making experience underscores two key aspects of his politics as an artist: one, that he and others from the artist collective try to diminish social hierarchies between artists and community members, and two, that by working to erase this artist-community member divide, he had an eye-opening revelation about the meaning of the term "postconflict" for this community. In addition, the mural project organically represented the community's perspective rather than being an imposition by the artists interpreting their pain, trauma, and suffering.

I was able to see Museo Itinerante for myself when I attended the Lima conference where I met Kristell (see Chapter 2). A large sign posted at the entrance to the museum described the exhibit in the following way:

[A] traveling museography without form, without defined space, without doors or walls, a space that collects the different memories which have been produced from art—in its various technologies and formats—about the years of violence in Peru.[20]

Given its mobility, this museum can appear in diverse locations, from "a plaza, a park, a classroom, a cultural centre or in any place." The artists' desire for this kind of flexibility is a way to "activate in the ordinary citizen, reflections, discussions, and opinions about a painful period of our history that has left large debts outstanding from the state and society to those who were victims." The artists extend an invitation to look and feel the stories and the diverse memories contained in the drawings, the artistic boards from Sarhua, graphics, installations, photographs and paintings, as these stories are testimonies that bring us closer to understanding our history and reconstruction of our own memory.

It is through this invitation that the artists of Museo Itinerante hope to create an exhibit space for, as their display sign stated, "an intercultural dialogue that brings together the memories of popular artists, urban artists, victims and activists who have made use of the symbolic resource to resist forgetting." Museo Itinerante is about a convergence of memories, from people in remote communities to those affected by violence in Lima. These artists are striving to reach an understanding of this difficult history by maintaining a sustained critique of social exclusion.

In seeking to bring communities together in an intercultural dialogue, the traveling nature of this museum is conducive to ensuring that these dialogues are decentralized (i.e., do not take place only in Lima). When I toured the exhibit in Lima, I was struck by how all the different features of this traveling museum—the photos, *retablos*, paintings, clay projects, and posters—came together in a beautiful and powerful montage. It felt like an intercultural dialogue of the heart, viewing work produced by a range of people using different aesthetic mediums and methods.

One of the most compelling aspects of this counterpublic is its artistic heterogeneity. Drawing from different art mediums and incorporating multiple memories, the traveling museum and its affiliated artists are part of a counterpublic that understands that multiple forms of artistic engagement are needed to reach the widest possible viewership and to facilitate the broadest forms of expression. For example, while photography may resonate with one set of viewers or affected community members, perhaps the narrative quilts resonate with another. In any case, the best kind of art provokes discussions that have previously been suppressed. By bringing together diverse artists and activists in a traveling exhibit as the basis for an intercultural dialogue, Museo Itinerante is advancing the idea that transitional justice art belongs everywhere because the impact was felt everywhere, and thus the restoration of fragmented communities must occur everywhere too.

Another important aspect of this art exhibit is its engagement with different memories, which acknowledges that multiple intercultural dialogues must occur as part of transitional justice. This point is especially relevant when we consider that those affected by the violence are extremely varied—from the rural campesino farmer to the urban union activist to the leftist student. The importance of sustaining multiple and simultaneous conversations about memories pertaining to the internal conflict suggests that resisting the desire to forget means having to navigate these various conversations without producing a hierarchy for the dialogue. Simply focusing on former president Fujimori's regime or on the disproportionate level of violence by Sendero Luminoso is not the goal. These artists and the Museo Itinerante artwork encourage various conversations, including those about Fujimori and Sendero Luminoso, simultaneously and in tension.

The act of recovering and uncovering memories from a counterpublic perspective garners new insights. Consider, for example, the posters designed by artist Mauricio Delgado Castillo titled "Un Dia Como Hoy" (A Day Like Today) that were part of Museo Itinerante when I visited.[21] These powerful posters highlight events of significance that correspond to the internal conflict period. As Mauricio describes it, this project is an intervention for Limeños that serves as a virtual calendar within the space of "non-physical memory" as a way of recovery, and of rejecting indifference and a desire to forget the atrocities of the internal conflict. The poster in Figure 2.1 documents the day when twelve women from Cusco arrived in Lima to denounce the forced sterilization campaign targeting Andean women under the Fujimori regime, as part of the longtime campaign led by the Asociación de Mujeres Peruanas Afectadas por las Esterilizaciones Forzadas (Association of Peruvian Women Affected by Forced Sterilization, AMPAEF). This struggle for recognition continues, as Mauricio was painting a new banner with AMPAEF for forcibly sterilized women in 2022 titled "Verdad, Justicia, y Reparación" (Truth, Justice, and Reparation), the three tenets of their ongoing campaign.[22]

Importantly, Mauricio engages in a significant exercise of visibility—the poster includes the names of the twelve women who arrived in Lima to demand justice on September 6, 2001, and highlighted AMPAEF's campaign. The sterilization campaigns under Fujimori are believed to have affected close to three hundred thousand women and twenty-one thousand men.[23] They occurred during the 1990s, specifically from 1996 to 1998.[24] Maricio's work highlights this state campaign of gender-based violence, which, upon first glance, might seem disconnected from the internal conflict. However, the state waged the sterilization campaign, which disproportionately targeted women, against rural and isolated Andean communities as one component of its multiple and aggressive strategies during the internal conflict. The forcible sterilization campaign then becomes another dimension to the internal conflict, rooted in social hierarchies of race, gender, and class that interact with a confluence of racism and patriarchy and that disproportionately affect poor communities. The description accompanying the poster not only engenders an image of these women as victims but also recognizes their agency in denouncing the state and forming AMPAEF, an association for forcibly sterilized women in search of accountability.

Due to the artists' stated intention of including diverse art creators, Museo Itinerante strives for memory portraits from a counterpublic perspective. It

Figure 2.1. A poster of the "Un Día Como Hoy" campaign to raise awareness about the effects of the internal conflict. This poster depicts the day that twelve women who were forcibly sterilized came from Cusco to Lima to demand justice.

grapples with the multiple social actors and deep layers of state complicity that problematically result in state violence, including the forcible sterilization campaigns, as necessary during these years of political upheaval. An intercultural dialogue between viewer and artworks and between artist and the reclamation of the right to memory is fundamental to the creation of transitional justice art.

Museo Itinerante is a powerful traveling exhibit in which artists have created a space for those affected to express their stories, suffering, and hopes for all to see. Viewers are then asked to reckon with those stories, those truths. The mobility of this museum is a striking feature because these stories should not be compartmentalized and they should occupy multiple spaces of social life. Through this model, an active human rights memory is born that viewers must respect and engage. Through this activation, uncomfortable dialogues can ensue, which is the only path for transformative memory to emerge.

Conclusion

The purpose of this chapter is to address how memory recovery creates the foundation from which transformative memory can became possible one day. Since the dominant public strives to endorse a primary narrative about the internal conflict that reveals a disdain for the lives lost, the purpose of public art and human rights education is to offer an important and creative counternarrative that can involve reclaiming public space for the purposes of openly and explicitly confronting the causes of sociopolitical violence, in the case of El Ojo Que Llora. The communities that gathered for Jorge at El Ojo Que Llora and the participants in the Memory Game should be considered as counterpublics because of their seeming willingness to search for complex truths. Without counterpublics, societies remain indoctrinated with dominant narratives about the internal conflict that benefit the elite minority.

Public art is a critical mechanism with which to cultivate the fostering of a human rights culture and to expand the meaning of transitional justice itself. Thus, having a public space to grieve, process and reflect, and even celebrate in community is essential. El Ojo Que Llora is an ideal site for commemorating the lives affected by violence during the internal conflict, with a recognition that those lives were also linked to a generation and legacy of pain. Relatedly, this memorial site fosters an environment for memory recovery.

The Memory Game is another community-centered way to approach memory recovery. Its importance lies in the various stages through which it takes participants—from recollection to vision. The Memory Game puts into practice Facing History's pedagogical triangle engaging heart, mind, and ethics as it asks participants to engage all three throughout. Of particular interest is how projects like the Memory Game cultivate a space of openness and nonjudgment. In what ways can people learn from this approach to reach another level of the conversation, to then imagine our collective futures? Moreover, how does decolonial feminism offer the conditions in which to capture effectively the relational ontologies that may be difficult (or even impossible) to understand in a nonlinear way? How can we recognize the knowledge production that comes forth through the queries of the game itself? If we understand knowledge production as a group endeavor, then that collective spirit can actually produce memories that we cannot conjure alone.

For the cultural shift to occur, human rights activists and artists cannot simply speak within their own communities. For a cultural shift to flourish, different kinds of people need to be engaged, beyond the social circles usually assembled. Art can be an important method or vehicle with which to open those spaces of conversation for healing, for remembering, and for cultivating a human rights culture and even signaling a dismantling of the tiers of citizenship that are deeply embedded in Peruvian society. For fundamental social change to take hold, transitional justice cannot be solely focused on carceral forms of accountability.

The traveling museum contributes to a process of memory recovery in which stories are told through different modalities and from a counterpublic perspective. The museum's intention of engaging memory everywhere and with everyone underscores the extent and breadth of the work that must be done. The critical need to expand the spaces in which these dialogues occur cannot be overstated. A project like Museo Itinerante is effective precisely because its method is to "activate" people, and it is this very instigation that will result in the emergence of transformative memory.

CHAPTER 3

No Somos Invisibles

Domestic Workers and La Casa de Panchita

The struggle for transitional justice in the aftermath of the internal conflict resulted in openings for more robust counterpublics to flourish. For example, the artistic depictions and memorials of the violence became more prominent, as I discussed in prior chapters. NGOs and labor organizations also began to proliferate, such as the Asociación Grupo de Trabajo Redes (AGTR, The Group Association of Labor Networks), of which La Casa de Panchita—the domestic worker rights organization I discuss in this chapter—is a part. In addition, laws more friendly to workers, such as the Domestic Workers Law of 2003, were passed in an effort to rebuild the social fabric of basic rights.

And yet, even in this struggle for transitional justice, for an end to impunity, and for a reckoning with the violence of the internal conflict, a parallel or related question remained for me: how might displaced Indigenous and campesina women fit into a pathway of transitional justice in their daily lives? To explore that question, I thought about Indigenous and campesina women working in the highly exploitative vocation of domestic work. As I argued in prior chapters, liberal reforms are certainly an improvement over state-sanctioned violence and civil war. And yet, in Perú, where centuries of colonialism and anti-Indigenous racial capitalism have yet to be fully confronted, and thus where tiers of citizenship remain in place, how do the women structurally subordinated near the bottom of the social hierarchy benefit? What institutions or movements inside Perú struggle with and for them? As artists contend with the violence of the recent (and at times, colonial) past, were activists or other civil society advocates similarly working toward a future free of structural violence for Indigenous and campesina women domestic workers?

In discussing the work of La Casa de Panchita (hereafter Panchita), I contend that this organization meaningfully contributes to the growth of a human rights counterpublic in the aftermath of the conflict. This is not a policy advocacy or a traditional political activist association, but rather an organization seeking to create labor relationships of dignity, and it does so among women across class, racial, ethnic, linguistic, and geographic lines. Its work is contributing to what I believe is a culture of human rights, where dignity, justice, and fairness become the cultural norms. This kind of work contributes to the transformative memory that I've been discussing throughout this book—Panchita's work involves asking for a new labor relationship to be realized that is not based on exploitation but rather on treating people and their work with dignity. I argue that they accomplish this, in part, by acknowledging the "complex personhood"[1] (discussed below) of each woman and by doing so in ways that recognize their daily labor conditions and relationships to community, including in regard to the relationships domestic workers have with their adolescent daughters. This latter project, discussed in this chapter, signals a commitment to human rights futures and to cultural transformation away from violence, patriarchy, and racism and toward dignity and rights.

During my several trips to Perú as a child and on into adulthood, it was impossible to ignore who was performing the domestic labor in the homes of family members and family friends—Indigenous or campesina women. As I uneasily witnessed the exchanges between employers and employees—too often very condescending—in the intimate space of the home, I started to consider how the interaction of global capitalism and white supremacy structured this tier of citizenship between them, especially in a racialized gendered way.

I remember observing uncomfortable exchanges between domestic workers and family members (i.e., stern voices directed at these women about their allegedly subpar job performance) and genuine curiosity from family members when I would try to talk with domestic workers about their lives. I still remember getting to know Consuelo during my dissertation research trip in the early 2000s when she worked for my aunt and uncle, and giving her my leftover food items as I was returning to the United States. She nearly cried at what I considered a simple gesture of not wanting to waste food. She hugged me and said, "I will miss you." I remember thinking I would miss her too, as she was so sweet and kind to me during my several weeks there. Consuelo was from southern Perú and she had been in Lima for about ten years by the time we met in the early 2000s. She was mother to a young child too. Some years later in 2010 I would see Consuelo again, now at my cousin's house. My cousin had not told me that Consuelo was now working for her family, so we were genuinely surprised to see each other. Consuelo said, "I'm so happy to see you. Your cousin didn't tell me you were here." I sighed, realizing my extended family did not appreciate how close I had gotten to Consuelo during my previous trip. Even though our reunion was brief, the joy we both felt upon seeing each other after so long is seared in my memory.

I emailed La Casa de Panchita in 2009 asking if it would be possible to arrange a meeting the following summer, as I had plans to travel to Lima. I was pleasantly surprised to receive a prompt response back from the executive director that Panchita would be open to my visit and would even permit me to conduct research with the organization. In the summer of 2010, I traveled to Lima and engaged in participant observation and informal interviews with the participants and staff of Panchita. I would return to conduct research with the organization for three additional summers.

Panchita opened its doors in January 2007 and is primarily an employment agency, and an important service that the organization provides to the community is as a contract negotiator. Prospective employers go to Panchita, detail their service needs, and then sign a contract with Panchita. Panchita identifies a domestic worker from its roster and matches her with the family. If for some reason the match does not work, the organization tries again. The benefit of this service is that the terms of agreement are made up front, and the domestic worker is not alone in negotiating a contract, which minimizes the prospect of abuse or exploitation and clarifies expectations. According to Panchita, this is how you treat work with dignity and advance a discourse about women's labor as being skilled. As previously mentioned, Panchita is part of the AGTR, which celebrated its twenty-fifth anniversary in 2023.

As an organization, Panchita did not see the women who walked through its doors as helpless victims but rather as having agency through which they could embody the capacity to assert their rights in a line of work where exploitation and abuse had been the norm for generations. It wanted to support these women in learning about their rights as stipulated by the Domestic Workers Law (Ley de las trabajadoras y trabajadores del hogar) of 2003 so that they could lead better lives and engage in dignified work, meaning that they would receive basic workers' rights such as time off, benefits, and limited hours of work per day and experience a work environment free from abuse, violence, racism, and sexual harassment. The Domestic Workers Law has since been updated in October 2020, improving many aspects of the 2003 law with regard to hiring contracts in writing, paid parental leave, and protection from multiple forms of discrimination.[2]

The disparate power relationship that exists between employer and domestic worker employee is facilitated by the lack of formal regulation. This dynamic is not unique to Perú but rather is part of a global pattern of exploitation that is deeply gendered and racialized. In Latin America, over 90 percent of the domestic work is performed by women.[3] And in the case of Perú, domestic work is primarily performed by Indigenous or campesina women. Thus, given the ethnic composition of this particular labor relationship—usually a mestizo/a employer and an Indigenous or campesina employee—it would be problematic to view this relationship in an ahistorical manner, disassociated from the legacies of sociracial hierarchies wherein elites viewed Indigenous and campesino peoples as "backward" and lacking the ability or capacity to contribute to Peruvian society and undeserving of full citizenship.

The sociopolitical unrest of the 1980s that stemmed from the internal conflict produced a situation in which rural communities were being forcibly and internally displaced. Some settled in nearby towns and villages or cities, including Lima. Finn Stepputat and Ninna Nyberg Sørensen write, "By the mid-1990s, between 300,000 and 600,000 people had been internally displaced."[4] The category of internally displaced people has not been embraced by these communities because of the deep stigma associated with being displaced: "As in most other situations where displacement takes place, it has been dangerous to be associated with the armed conflict in Peru, and to be 'desplazado' meant to be poor, destitute, marginal, uneducated and rural. People who were eager to become socially mobile, and particularly those who had previous urban links and experience, would therefore not readily identify themselves as desplazados."[5] This hesitation has everything to do with being associated with terrorism because of where the members of these communities lived prior to their displacement. In other words, a concern about being labeled as *terrucos*, as terrorists, always lingers once they enter Lima.

Starting in the 1980s, the forced and voluntary migration of many people from rural communities making their way to Lima was a result of the internal conflict.[6] Young girls who arrived in Lima sought employment as domestic workers and settled in the outskirts, which resulted in an explosive growth of homes in the city margins. The first domestic workers' rights reform legislation introduced in the 1980s did not move forward. Another attempt was made in 1994 during the Fujimori administration; even though Congress approved it, Fujimori rejected it. And then, "twenty-three years after the first bill was submitted, a watered-down legislative bill that partially equalized domestic workers' rights with those of other workers was finally approved in 2003."[7]

In this chapter, we see that the assertion of domestic workers' rights in Lima is part of the internal conflict aftermath story. These workers are a reflection of the tiers of citizenship; thus, a social reconciliation must take place as part of transitional justice efforts, and this can occur only by addressing structural labor inequalities throughout the country. In response to this citizenship tier, organizations such as Panchita are working at the intersection of race, gender, and class status. As Merike Blofield argues, the 2003 Domestic Workers Law is imperfect and offers only partial protections, though some of these flaws have been rectified in the updated law that went into effect in April 2021.[8] Panchita offers important workshops to inform domestic workers of the basic tenets of the legal protections enacted through the law, producing a context in which domestic workers know their legal rights.

In this chapter, I discuss the Panchita workshops I observed, the informal interviews I did with domestic workers there, Panchita's contract negotiation services, and its program to break the generational cycle of exploitation of girls. All of this work contributes to a counterpublic that is directly oppositional to a dominant status quo that relies on racialized gendered exploitation and enforces tiers of citizenship in which rural communities are further isolated when they enter urban spaces. In Lima the employer–domestic worker employee dynamic is haunted by legacies of racialized gendered social violence, including from Spanish colonialism.

Domestic work is extremely devalued and has not been seen as legitimate work, which made instituting even modest legal protections enormously difficult. Indigenous communities have historically been marginalized as noncitizens in Perú, meaning that they do not experience legal rights in the same way as other Peruvians and thus their *deservingness* of legal protections has yet to be fully recognized. Moreover, legal protections are not sufficient if they are not enforced. Alongside enforcement, a cultural shift is needed in this relationship of unequal power, wherein the norms, values, and ideologies about Indigenous or campesino communities, and women in particular, change radically. A focus on the advocacy role of Panchita shows that this cultural shift must center the workers and remake an elite political landscape that for too long has viewed Indigenous or campesino communities as "Other" and as noncitizens, resulting in a cultural devaluation of their existence and labor. In their self-advocacy, these domestic workers are asking to be seen, to be really seen, in a way that undermines the interplay of social violence, race, and citizenship.

Specters of Haunting

As sociologist Avery F. Gordon writes, "Even those who live in the most dire circumstances possess a complex and oftentimes contradictory humanity and subjectivity that is never adequately glimpsed by viewing them as victims or, on the other hand, as superhuman agents."⁹ Gordon seeks a messier portrayal not only of people themselves but also of power—which is sometimes obvious and oftentimes obscure—and, specifically, the haunting ghosts. She states, "Complex personhood means that even those called 'Other' are never *never* that" (emphasis added).¹⁰ When seeing the totality of people—arguably their complex humanity—no one benefits from a "pure victim" framework. Social life, as Gordon argues, is far more intricate, and the difficulty has a lot to do with the ghosts being ignored:

> Haunting is not the same as being exploited, traumatized, or oppressed, although it usually involves these experiences or is produced by them. What's distinctive about haunting is that it is an animated state in which a repressed or unresolved social violence is making itself known, sometimes very directly, sometimes more obliquely. I use the term *haunting* to describe those singular yet repetitive instances when home becomes unfamiliar, when your bearings on the world lose direction, when the over-and-done-with comes alive, when what's been in your blind spot comes to view. Haunting raises specters, and it alters the experience of being in time, the way we separate the past, the present, and the future.¹¹

I started to think about Gordon's conceptualization of "complex personhood" and of haunting with regard to the domestic workers from my research. How should I understand this haunting, this uncomfortable, uneasy, and disquieting reality of social violence that seems to permeate all aspects of Peruvian life, including domestic work? What is this "unresolved social violence [that] is making itself known" through the fissures that have become exposed during the years of internal conflict but are in no way bound to this temporality? And, even more profoundly, how do I understand the way exploited women also harm and traumatize others? In this way, colonialism is social violence, which is not necessarily a new contention, but the legacy of colonialism must underscore that the generational harm is found everywhere and in all directions.

Colonialism as social violence is also associated with authoritarianism. The roots of this authoritarianism are linked to the country's military dictatorships dating back to 1968, and even further back, to the early twentieth century, when Perú actively engaged in the project of industrialization.¹² Industrialization became about modernity, and modernity is social violence. Hence, the haunting of industrialization is about the oppressive or dominant power that elites exerted in trying to suppress subversive logics starting in the early twentieth century.

As historian Paulo Drinot argues, "Both the idea that industrialization was equivalent to civilization and progress and in turn the idea that labor was a valuable resource that needed to be protected and enhanced because it was essential to the project of industrialization were inflated locally by Peru's particular social and cultural configurations; namely, by the fact that Peru's predominately white elites viewed the country's predominately indigenous population as culturally and racially backward and as an obstacle to progress."[13] The industrialization period meant that domestic work would never be seen as recognizable labor, as having value, because it was not in service of the civilizing mission of industrialization. Here Drinot makes another important contention—another haunting, if you will—about citizenship. In this period of industrialization the elite view was that Indigenous peoples did not merit or deserve citizenship; this was a privilege for whites or mestizos who were willing participants and ideal messengers of the industrialization project. Industrial labor was progress, and the only ones who could engage in this progress were non-Indigenous peoples.

This context is relevant to the haunting because the common understanding of why the internal conflict went on as long as it did is that the state ignored Indigenous peoples. But Drinot offers a more complicated portrait about the exclusion of Indigenous peoples. He argues, "The exclusion of the Indian from projects of nation-state formation was not the consequence of the Peruvian state's 'failures,' as is often argued. Rather the exclusion of the Indian has been and is immanent to the project of Peruvian nation-state formation, which was and in many ways continues to be premised on the *overcoming* of indigeneity, that is to say on the de-Indianization of Peru."[14] From this premise of de-Indianization, scholars and historians argue the Peruvian nation-state formed as a "weak state."[15]

The state was weak not only because it excluded the majority population in the country but also because it failed to establish a strong state bureaucracy and institutions throughout the country. If the goal for elites was the de-Indianization of the country, then neglecting rural parts of the country would help achieve that goal. What is the incentive for integrating Indigenous peoples into or including them in this formation if they represented a lack of progress? In other words, citizenship by birth was irrelevant to elites; citizenship by race became the metric by which to establish the country. In Perú, the context for understanding race and racism involves mestizos, who emphasize their European heritage from Spain; Indigenous, Andean, Amazonian, and campesino communities that do not have a real or even an imagined connection to Spain; and other non-mestizo-identified people, such as those of African or Asian descent. Race operates far more fluidly in Perú than it does in the United States, and therefore the process of racialization in Latin America is a contemporary reflection of colonial markers.

The lack of an infrastructure to protect domestic workers should be tied to the prior decades that disproportionately devalued labor done by Indigenous or campesino communities. Returning to Gordon's earlier points, then, "How do we reckon with what modern history has rendered ghostly? How do we develop a critical language to describe and analyze the affective, historical, and mnemonic structures of such haunting?"[16] Resolving this quandary is difficult, because the existing language of reparation and restorative justice feels inadequate, and in essence limits concepts of transitional justice. While both are important processes, they do not fully "reckon with" the ghosts of coloniality, violence, and repression. If haunting is about specters that convolute one's sense of time and home, then the internal conflict is the epitome of this haunting—the centrality of social violence that is demanding to be seen. This social violence is about neglect, exclusion, racism, colonialism, patriarchy, sexual violence, abuse, brutality, Eurocentrism, and so forth.

Another haunting that pervades this employer–domestic worker employee relationship is the civilizing mission. This is in part linked to Catholicism, but it is also about Peruvian elites who deemed Indigenous or campesino peoples—from the Andes to the Amazon—as needing to be "civilized." It is precisely this eugenicist logic of civilizing that empowered President Alberto Fujimori to forcibly sterilize thousands of Indigenous women without their knowledge or full understanding.[17] How could an "uncivilized" woman give consent? Since she cannot give consent, there is no need to inform her of what is happening to her own body. As has been widely reported now, the doctors performing these procedures insulted the women using racist and ethnic slurs, or outright lied to them about their health needs. Interestingly, the Asociación de Mujeres Peruanas Afectadas por las Esterilizaciones Forzadas (the Association of Peruvian Women Affected by Forcible Sterilization), the advocacy group seeking accountability for forced sterilization under the Fujimori regime, has an office based in San Juan de Miraflores in Lima, where Panchita also has a small outpost for its girls' program. So the overlap between victims of forced sterilization, displaced communities, and future domestic workers collide in this district.

The German sociologist Encarnación Gutiérrez Rodríguez states the following about a decolonial approach to the feminization of labor related to domestic work and affect, which "carries residues of meaning": "They are haunted by past intensities, not always spelled out and conceived in the present. Immediate expressions and transmissions of affects may indeed revive repressed sensations, experiences of pain or joy. Although not explicitly expressed as such, they are temporal and spatial constellations of certain times, intricately impressed in legacies of the past and itineraries of the present/future."[18] Long-lasting racist and patriarchal logics about Indigenous or campesina women result in justifying their exploitation. The specter of haunting permeates an employer–domestic worker employee relationship that existed during the internal conflict, specifically in terms of the apathy shown toward those being disproportionately and directly affected. The employer-employee relationship is shaped by a legacy that cannot be ignored, and has been present through every interaction since the Spanish conquest. The 2003 Domestic Workers Law was a small step toward addressing a generational problem in which domestic workers who are mostly Indigenous have been treated as noncitizens for too long.

Panchita's Workshops

The passage of the 2003 Domestic Workers Law provided minimal regulations, and in Perú, as in other countries, there is differential treatment between live-in domestic workers and non-home-based domestic workers. Those who lived in the home were often subject to endless work hours and tasked with jobs that went above and beyond why they were initially hired. Employers often took advantage of the fact that the workers' family members would not be nearby. In the 1980s, the maximum number of work hours per week for workers in Perú, excluding domestic workers, was forty-eight hours; for domestic workers, it was ninety-six hours. Domestic workers labored nearly twice as many hours per week as workers in other sectors. By 2010, the weekly hours for domestic workers were reduced to forty-eight and matched those of other Peruvian workers.[19]

As a result of the passage of the 2003 legislation, eight-hour workdays totaling forty-eight-hour work weeks with one day off per week became the legal standard. Domestic workers were to receive paid vacation of fifteen days (other workers get more vacation days), were entitled to two weeks of severance pay, and had a right to a social security pension. However, domestic workers did not have a minimum wage, as did other workers. Even though domestic workers had a right to social security, many did not understand the process for establishing this pension. In an environment of "chronic informality," the percentage of domestic workers that know about these rights is quite low, with only 3.7 percent of workers having established state pensions by 2008.[20] The challenge of reaching prospective domestic workers to inform them about these legal rights is an enormous one that organizations such as Panchita have taken on.

The 2003 law contains a series of provisions that Panchita reviews in detail in its workshops. These provisions include a confidentiality clause (article 4); ensuring acceptable living conditions, which does not include a monthly or weekly wage, unlike other jobs (article 5); instituting a wage schedule to provide consistent payment (article 6); a fifteen-day minimum for giving notice that applies to both the employer and the employee (article 7); an explanation of the process of termination when it comes to an unexpected death (article 8); and detailing the social benefits that now apply to domestic workers (articles 9, 11, 12, 13, and 18).

Employers had politically pressured Fujimori to reject the Domestic Workers Law when it crossed his desk. This was in 1993, when the country was still in upheaval following Fujimori's self-coup and his attempts to embolden his authoritarian regime while being on the cusp of launching the forced sterilization campaigns. The legislation remained stalled in Congress until 2003 during the Toledo administration. In that year, about eight versions of the proposal had been put forth by different congressional representatives. In the end, the signed legislation took up various aspects of all of these different proposals.

Open during the day Sunday through Thursday, Panchita works with child, youth, and adult domestic workers; it is a place for them to learn about their rights, find secure employment opportunities through Panchita's employment placement unit, and gain concrete skills to do their jobs better and more efficiently. Panchita is located in the district of Jesús María, about twenty minutes from the apartment I rented in Miraflores. It offers education workshops (including cooking and first aid), legal training, work counseling, and even psychological therapy. I assisted and observed the child rearing and legal training workshops and, when possible, assisted and observed the Sunday workshops.

To describe Panchita as a domestic workers' rights organization may be inadequate. Panchita is an organization that addresses the "complex personhood" of participants by engaging them and their needs from a place of compassion and respect. Panchita's advocacy work is in trying to rewrite the tired script of exploitation by working closely with participants and their families to create a more stable future. The work is extremely challenging, especially when working with women who may still be dealing with the hardships of being internally displaced.

In mid-June 2010 I met with Panchita's volunteer coordinator. We arranged a work volunteer schedule that aligned with my daughter's daycare hours. In appreciation for the organization giving me the space and opportunity to conduct research, I agreed to do online searches for possible funding sources and do English translations of its reports to foreign funders about the effects and impact of Panchita's programmatic work. The volunteer coordinator introduced me to her coworkers, and I had a chance to just hang out in the main waiting room area. My daughter, then three years old, was with me on my first visit to Panchita. I noticed all of the signs promoting the 2003 Domestic Workers Law in the lobby, Law 27986, *Ley de la trabajadora del hogar*. Throughout this main lobby area were large banners and other posters about labor rights. I even noticed a larger banner promoting an international conference of domestic workers from the Americas that stated "*No somos invisibles*" (We are not invisible), which serves as a motto for this work. Panchita has a very inviting and warm atmosphere. Someone sits at the front desk near the front door ready to greet you; the large waiting area has high ceilings and comfortable couches arranged in a rectangle facing each other. The waiting room has adequate light and the staircase to the second floor has a vintage feel.

I began my research at Panchita by observing the childcare workshop. The childcare session took place in a makeshift room on the building's roof. Attendance at these various workshops can vary—the one on this particular day had two participants, Maria and Celinda. Lilly, a Panchita staff member and trained psychologist, facilitated this childcare workshop. Lilly said that two was a pretty low number and that her workshops can have as many as twelve participants. Panchita has a community rule that everyone goes by their first name to establish a community feel—no "Senora" salutations take place here.

Maria was very soft-spoken and originally came from Cusco. She mentioned that she had come to Panchita in search of a job and to possibly participate in some trainings when her schedule permitted. She had been employed as a live-in domestic worker at a home in Lima, and was given two days' notice of the termination of her employment. As the mother of a twelve-year-old daughter at the time, she was visibly upset while telling the group her story. She had been distraught at receiving the news that she was out of a job, and in forty-eight hours would no longer even have a place to live. Her boss replied, "What are you so upset about? You have two more days of food and shelter." Maria could not believe she could be fired in this way. She told us, "*Me sentí desesperada*" (I felt desperate).

By the time of the workshop, Maria still did not have a job, and she did not disclose where she was living with her daughter. She shared with us that she had come to Panchita quite some time ago for a workshop but had not thought of Panchita as a resource for her. But then her job situation suddenly changed with her no longer being employed, and then she found a small Panchita flyer in her wallet. She knew she had to reach out to the organization again and was now hoping to secure a safe and reliable job.

Celinda's situation was very different. Not only was she extremely talkative, with numerous stories to share (that sometimes derailed the training), but she had her own residence near the airport. As the mother of three daughters and the grandmother of several grandchildren, she disclosed that several of those grandchildren were living with her at the moment. Celinda had heard about Panchita from a friend, who encouraged her to attend the workshops. Celinda did not disclose any other reason for attending the workshop other than that her friend had encouraged her to do so. She did share with the group that one of her grandchildren was very challenging and demanding; it seemed as if she was at a loss as to how to handle this child.

Even though the training took place in a makeshift room on the roof of the building, Lilly started the session by talking about the importance of space, of decorating and personalizing it to create an inviting place. It was easy to tell that this was the room where childcare workshops were held—it featured nursery décor with lots of stuffed animals and baby dolls, and was painted bright yellow. As Lilly pointed out the yellow paint and the child decorations and posters, she admitted that the room would be pretty drab and would actually feel like a shack if it had not been spruced up. She then compared decorating this meeting space to decorating one's living space. Even for a live-in domestic worker with tiny living quarters, it was important to claim space and place.

After Lilly distributed some reading materials and asked us each to introduce ourselves to the group in the front of the room (Celinda went first, then Maria, and then myself), Lilly asked that we provide the speaker with a positive comment or affirmation after they finished speaking. It was an ice-breaker exercise to help the participants feel comfortable and ready to engage and share. The workshop itself was quite interactive. We role-played handling difficult children who refused to go to bed or take medication, for example. Given Lilly's background as a psychologist, she spoke at great length about how childhood experiences affect our relationship with children as adults.

She specifically addressed the difficulties for Peruvians who grew up in the midst of terrorism, as they experienced so much violence from Sendero Luminoso and the state military. What kind of lasting damage has resulted from these internal conflict years, she pondered out loud. She mentioned that children often bear the brunt of adults' feelings of helplessness. For instance, if an employer is being mean, then we may channel our frustration toward our children, or even the elderly. She also connected the issue of family violence to our ability (or inability) to care for children.

As I reviewed my field notes about this training session, I wrote that I was struck with the fact that a workshop about childcare could be linked to the internal conflict. The trainer was referring to generational trauma—and that trauma stays with us over time. The internal conflict haunts people and generations even in spaces that are seemingly distant from the internal conflict. Linking trauma and violence to child rearing is powerful and reminds me of hearing Cherríe Moraga talk at a conference many years ago about not realizing she had passed on her anger to her own child.[21]

When I observed this same childcare and health workshop about two weeks later, in early July 2010, I saw Celinda and Maria in the waiting room. I waved to them and asked what they were up to that day. They were attending a different Panchita workshop. A participant must complete five all-day workshops in order to earn a certificate of completion, which could be appealing to prospective employers. This time, Lilly had seven women in her workshop. Though the content remained the same, it felt like a different workshop. It reminded me of my experience as a professor—same class but entirely different experience with new people. In both of these childcare workshops, Lilly had the participants engage in some exercises that involved reading aloud. Nearly all of the women had a difficult time completing this exercise. It would be apparent to anyone observing that they struggled with basic reading—in this case ordering healthy food from a menu. I enthusiastically participated in the exercise too, not realizing initially that others were struggling with the task.

Every one of these women came from a rural part of the country. Their personalities ranged from being quite timid to being very outspoken. Unlike Maria and Celinda, this group had a very difficult time offering compliments. It became awkward seeing how truly difficult it was for the women to compliment each other in this opening ice-breaker exercise. After a while, the compliments became repetitive, and an exercise that should have taken no more than twenty minutes lasted close to one hour.

Lilly started the training by observing that domestic workers' upbringing and childhood experiences inform the types of relationships they have with the children they care for at work, and even with their own children. As Lilly broached the topic of domestic violence and terrorism, this time it was the subject of family violence that lingered in this group's conversation. Everyone acknowledged having witnessed or experienced domestic violence. Lilly said, "When we ask Rosa, why the bruise, . . . she says, 'Well, I was clumsy and fell,' and then the next day she has a black eye and says, 'Well, a box hit me in the eye.' How many of us have heard stories like these?" Everyone nodded. "So we know that Rosa is not being honest, so then how does family violence affect our relationship with children, with others?" It was during this section of the training that one of the women,

Alejandra, had some questions for Lilly. She proceeded to describe a violent incident with her husband in which he pushed her while she had her baby with her. In response, she threw something back at him, perhaps a kitchen pot. Alejandra said this incident happened very early on in their nearly twenty-year marriage and that her husband had not raised a hand to her since this incident. She wanted to know if this was domestic violence, but Lilly was not sure what to call the incident other than to describe it as Alejandra reacting to protect herself and her baby. The group seemed to be processing all of this information from both Alejandra and Lilly, as these kinds of incidents were all too familiar.

In workshops about child rearing, the specters of violence are pervasive—from family violence to the internal conflict. These workshops interweave skills-building with deep reflection. Lilly managed to adjust the content based on the needs of the participants in the room. This approach underscores the emotional aspect of caring for children—if we carry trauma with us this can affect the younger generation. Moreover, unresolved trauma can also correspond to one's self-worth. In breaking this cycle of violence, acknowledging these haunting ghosts is a start.

In the workshops, Lilly also provided the participants with commonplace scenarios so that they could understand that their work had boundaries. She said domestic workers too often reported that the families they worked for added extra tasks to an already full schedule. She told them, "If you've been hired to watch the children, then you should not also agree to watch the cousins, for instance." Lilly said the adding on of tasks can start subtly. Before a domestic worker realizes it, they may find themselves doing all of the cooking, and then all of the laundry, when they were initially hired to care for an elderly relative. Lilly spent quite a bit of time talking to the women about being comfortable with sticking up for themselves, keeping their composure even when the employer did not keep hers (most of these women report to the wives in these homes), and simply and calmly reiterating that they did not agree in their contract to take on this additional labor. Lilly told them that once a door is opened, and they agree to accept additional tasks here and there, then it is only a matter of time before the amount of work will become unsustainable.

Many women shared that this scenario was one they knew all too well. Known as *servicio completo* (full service), domestic workers are hired to do everything—cooking, cleaning, and caring for kids, which is nearly impossible to do well all at once. Some shared how they would get in trouble with their employer and get scolded if anything went wrong. For instance, if something happened to the child, even though they had been ordered to prepare dinner and were unable to pay full attention to the child, the domestic workers would get in serious trouble. Everyone in the group had stories.

A couple of days later, I observed a different Panchita workshop, this one on caring for the elderly. Panchita staffer Leidy facilitated this session. Leidy is an extremely skilled facilitator, and I was grateful that she permitted me to sit in on the workshop. As I helped her prepare for the workshop (bringing in a portable bed, setting up the chairs in a U shape, grabbing miscellaneous items from throughout the office for the hands-on exercises), three women entered the room—two women named Maria and another woman named Rosa. I had seen and interacted with all of these women at Panchita before. Leidy began the workshop by talking about the three phases of change in elderly people—physical, psychological, and social—and covered topics such as menopause for women, andropause for men, and common illnesses affecting the elderly. As in the prior workshops, any kind of reading activity made apparent the participants' literacy challenges.

In late morning, the group took a short break. It was during these breaks that I could casually converse with the women about their lives. On this particular day, participants told me that their pay was between five hundred and seven hundred soles per month (about US$180–$250),[22] and that it really was the luck of the draw in terms of the employer's temperament, because they run the gamut. I asked one of the Marias if she had noticed improved working conditions since the passage of the 2003 Domestic Workers Law. She said absolutely, and that the changes were quite noticeable given what they and others had experienced before. Rosa emphatically agreed. As I continued to talk with Maria and Rosa, we had the following exchange:

> **ROSA:** So where are you from?
> **ME:** I'm from the United States.
> **ROSA:** Wow, it is beautiful there, right? That's what I hear.
> **ME:** Some parts nice, some parts not so nice. Just like everywhere.
> **MARIA #1:** I heard it is really nice. A family member of mine went there. I don't know where—and she said it is really nice.
> **ME:** Well, yes, many parts are nice.
> **MARIA #1:** You must have a domestic worker there then.
> **ME:** Actually, I don't. We try to do everything on our own: caring for the house, our child, and working full-time. It is a lot, but no, I don't have a domestic worker, actually.

Both Rosa and Maria seemed genuinely surprised that I did not have a domestic worker, especially once they heard I worked full-time outside of the home.

> **ROSA:** (*jokingly*) Are you interested in one from here? Like me!

No Somos Invisibles

All three of us laughed. I remember that exchange like it happened yesterday. I finally had to ask myself why it stayed with me so long, this seemingly innocuous conversation. In retrospect, the privilege of being from the United States had entered the conversation. The exchange also revealed how the exploitation of US domestic workers is so hidden from global view. The fact that US domestic workers are predominantly immigrant women of color has meant that their abuse and exploitation could be compounded by their legal status. Because of the rampant exploitation, the United States has long been trying to pass legal protections for domestic workers.[23]

After realizing that it was taking me a long time to get to Panchita in the morning and even longer to get to my daughter's daycare in the afternoon, I asked the women how long it took them to get to Panchita for these workshops, which began at 9:30 a.m. The amount of time for the three of them to travel to Panchita ranged from ninety minutes to over two hours. One of the Marias told me she left her home at 7 a.m. in order to make it on time. She usually arrived around 9:15. She lives in Villa El Salvador with her twelve-year-old daughter. When Maria, who was originally from Cusco, was eight months pregnant, her daughter's father left the family.

Another Panchita workshop I observed focused on the environment and home emergencies. I knew all eight of the women in this workshop from prior Panchita workshops. The workshop was led by Rachel, a white woman who was a longtime volunteer from New York City. Compared to the other two workshops I had observed, this was the most political. The first half of the workshop focused on the environment, and the second half focused on home emergencies and accidents.[24]

Rachel led the group through a wide-ranging discussion about the environment. She asked each of the women where they were from if not from Lima. None had been born in Lima, and the vast majority came from places I had never heard of. All of them currently lived in the outskirts of Lima. After these casual introductions, Rachel then talked about global warming, water wars, waste, recycling, carbon dioxide, and other environmental matters. She had a handmade quilt with felt images depicting global warming. This quilt showed the ozone layer and addressed its depletion. Much of what Rachel was saying about environmental changes resonated with the women; they commented on how they had noticed those changes in their homes of origin. Rachel was merely explaining the phenomenon that these women had been experiencing.

After the morning session we had a brief break, during which Alejandra told me she had quit her job taking care of an elderly man. I had met Alejandra during the childcare training, when she had been hoping to locate work quickly. She had found work, but the elderly man she was caring for kept asking her for a date. One night, he even entered her room. She had enough of the harassment and quit.

Performing domestic work can be quite dangerous, and emergency situations can arise. Rachel addressed emergencies and accidents such as choking, fire, getting burned, getting electrocuted, and falling on one's head. Rachel even shared that a previous participant had told them that her four-year-old nephew had died after swallowing a balloon. All of the women in the room had dealt with serious emergency situations. Even in cases where they were the ones personally injured, such as Maribel, who had gotten electrocuted, the employer showed no sympathy and ordered them back to work. The workshop reminded them that domestic workers performed skilled work that involved risks and therefore it was all the more pertinent they understood their legal rights.

I remember a day when the traffic to Miraflores was even heavier than usual and I almost did not make it on time to pick up my daughter from daycare. As I worried about the traffic and being late, I looked out the window and saw a domestic worker. We were driving through the elite district of San Isidro, where many US diplomats have their homes. She was on her knees, scrubbing the front door tile area of a home. I wondered why she was not using a mop—was she not permitted to do so, was this a power move to have her on her knees scrubbing the walkway? I'll never know the answer, but it felt like such a startling cognitive dissonance to have my thoughts disrupted from having just left a training with the intent of empowering domestic workers to witnessing this laborer on her hands and knees: invisible labor in plain sight of the elites in this district.

These workshops are about finding ways to empower domestic workers (either current or prospective) and to help them to not only understand the value and importance of their work but also acknowledge the challenges of this labor. It is not easy to calm a crying baby, to keep one's temper if a child is being disrespectful, or to keep at bay the traumas of childhood and youth that become ghosts in our adulthood. Yet by acknowledging the effects of the internal conflict, from its forcible displacement to its trauma, women participants are able to find new meaning in their lives.

Legal Rights and Empowering Girls

When I returned to Panchita in June 2012, things had changed. No longer were five all-day workshops required for certification. The requirement proved too taxing, and many women complained about the difficulty of attending so many trainings on successive days. Now only two days were required, and Panchita changed the curriculum to reflect more specialized training, such as cooking. During this research trip, I observed the law workshops and learned about the girls' program.

On the first day I observed the training, three women attended: Nelida, Ayde, and Doris.[25] Doris, a Mexican national working for a Peruvian family, was struggling to understand her situation and, more specifically, her rights as a domestic worker given that she was not a Peruvian citizen. Nelida was in her early forties and from Iquitos. Ayde was from Cusco. Both Nelida and Ayde had heard about the 2003 Domestic Workers Law but knew little about it.

Sofia, the facilitator of the law workshop, was a former domestic worker and now a Panchita staff member. She wanted to be sure the women understood every aspect of the law and their associated rights. Article 3 of the Domestic Workers Law states that a work contract is required; this can be either oral or written. Panchita stresses that written contracts are more effective. If an employer moves, then the employer must pay for the transportation of the domestic worker if the employee wants to retain her services. In explaining the different facets of a work contract, the Panchita staff told domestic workers that it was important and appropriate to ask questions about the contract. Domestic workers run into trouble when they make assumptions about sick leave, for instance, or do not retain a copy of the contract for their files. Panchita advised domestic workers to make three copies of the contract: one for the employer, one for the domestic worker, and one for Panchita to keep on file. With her previous employer, Ayde had no contract and worked from 8 a.m. to midnight.

Panchita offers services in which it acts as the mediator between the employer and the employee. Job interviews can take place at Panchita's offices. Each employer that goes through Panchita to hire a domestic worker agrees to a three-day paid work period for both parties to determine if a work situation is feasible. During this trial work period, the domestic worker is paid for the work, even if in the end she does not continue. If after the trial period both parties agree to continue, then on the fourth day a contract is signed in the presence of a Panchita representative. The employers are aware that a contract must be signed at Panchita on the fourth day. The organization emphasized that it is important for the domestic worker herself to read the contract and not to rely on the employer to read the contract to her. All of this information proved especially useful to Doris, who had no idea what rights she had as a Mexican national.

Panchita explained that there were two types of work contract available: *tiempo definido* (defined time), which has a clear start and end date, and *tiempo indefinido* (indefinite time), which has a start date but no end date. In general, most of the contracts fall into the latter category, but *tiempo definido* contracts can be common in cases in which a domestic worker is asked to relocate. Each of these contracts has different benefits. It is important to be clear about expectations and responsibilities. Employers who use Panchita's employment agency for their services pay S/.350 for the service;[26] it is unacceptable for employers to try to circumvent the Panchita protocol and sign a contract directly with a domestic worker without a Panchita representative present. The domestic workers are informed that should this happen, the employer is not following the mutually agreed rules, and they should refuse to sign a work contract with them.

Panchita's law training involved both a detailed explanation of the existing law and a rationale for the provision. For example, the confidentiality clause (article 4) is a reminder of the importance of being respectful of a family's privacy and that they too should be respectful of the worker's, with exceptions to the privacy clause for cases of abuse, family violence, or criminal activity. Another aspect of confidentiality concerns security. Domestic workers should not disclose details, even informally, about working alone during the day to friends. They must remember that even though they are working in a home, it is a workplace, and that their employers are not friends. If family violence occurs, a domestic worker is not obligated to report it but can call the Women's Ministry to file an anonymous report. Nelida disclosed that she had witnessed many incidents of family violence and had found that nothing could be done in those cases. Rape is also a very real threat facing domestic workers. Doris knew of a domestic worker who had been raped by her employer with no repercussions for the employer.

As previously mentioned, the Domestic Workers Law does not guarantee a minimum wage, but when an employer signs a work contract with Panchita they are (as of 2010) agreeing to an established minimum wage of S/.750 per month with benefits, just like other workers. Diana, who was Sofia's cofacilitator the day I attended the law workshop, said that it is important for domestic workers to have an idea of how much they want to earn with an accompanying rationale based on experience and job responsibilities. Diane said that entering a work contract without a clear idea about the desired wage would mean the employer would have the upper hand.

Many domestic workers reported cases of wage theft and sudden firings. The 2003 law addressed this too frequent reality by formulating a payment schedule and establishing a fifteen-day window for any changes to the employer-employee relationship (with the exception of death). Employers are under no obligation to tell you why you've been fired (*despido intempestivo*), but they are still bound to pay you for fifteen more days. The law's subsequent articles pertaining to social benefits meant that domestic workers could now have holiday breaks, vacation time, and a pension. To be entitled to the rights and benefits associated with the Domestic Workers Law, they must work at least four hours per day, Monday through Saturday, or the equivalent of twenty-four hours per week in the same home.

Legal protections play a role in building a human rights culture in Perú. As the Panchita organization seeks to inform the beneficiaries of these legal protections about their rights, the staff acknowledge that the enormous undertaking here cannot be resolved through workshops and their direct services alone. Undoing a generational culture of exploitation requires both working with current domestic workers as well as reaching adolescent girls to ensure they complete their schooling and even perhaps chart out a different future than their mothers.

Forging a Different Path: Working with Adolescent Girls

In early July 2010 I had a lengthy two-hour conversation with Ana Maria about an adolescent program in San Juan de Miraflores, which is located about thirty minutes outside of Lima, south of Surco, and is supported by a funder in Luxembourg.[27] We arranged for me to join her for a visit to the program site a couple of weeks after our meeting. The program called Apoyo para el Futuro (Support for the Future) was in its second year when I visited. Ana Maria works with adolescent girls ranging in age from eleven to sixteen, and every Sunday, Panchita offers self-esteem and education workshops. She said they had done two *jornados* (day gatherings) that year. The public education in this area, and in Lima in general, is atrocious, she told me.

The program has worked with between forty and sixty girls. One season they had up to ninety girls in attendance. Ana Maria told me, "If we can save at least ten of them, then it was worth the effort." By "saving" them she meant rescuing them from the life of exploitation, abuse, and violence experienced by their mothers. She shared that the difficulty of the program was accepting no viable option really existed for these poor girls: they are in dire conditions, with wild dogs running around their neighborhoods, and terrible sanitation, and they were extremely isolated. Based on her interaction with the girls, she said that the girls see domestic work as holding the promise of upward mobility. Life is hard for these families in general but is even more difficult for the girls, according to Ana Maria. The girls experience a tremendous amount of discrimination because of where they live. For instance, Panchita has a very difficult time contracting buses to pick up the girls and bring them to the organization for workshops or events.

At the time of this interview, the Panchita team of the girls' program consisted of four people, all university educated. The team had plans to design a research project assessment to better understand the girls' progress, if any. Panchita wanted to understand both the girls' and their mothers' views about their futures. At this particular site, Panchita workshops focused on self-esteem, educational games, reproductive rights, theater, and art. In May it was "Water Day," so Panchita organized an activity around water and had some powerful conversations with the girls on the topic. These workshops took place in the neighborhood's common dining hall area.

Some fathers at first resisted Panchita's efforts—these were the more "traditional" fathers who felt that their daughters should be home preparing their meals (i.e., "Who is going to cook for me?"). In order for a girl to participate in the program, at least one of her parents had to sign an agreement. Panchita relied on this agreement to tell the fathers that the girls could not leave the workshop. At first, the fathers were incensed: "Wait, this is my daughter. I want to get her now." But the staff kept bringing up the signed contract; the daughters were required to stay. The Panchita staff explained to the parents that the arrangement had been agreed to in advance. Eventually the fathers had to agree to uphold the contract. Ana Maria said that in the end, the majority of fathers are fine with the workshops; she estimated that about 90 percent of them are cooperative.

It is nearly impossible for the staff to not be involved in family problems at home. Even though they try very hard to create boundaries, these boundaries are not always maintained. In one case, a battered woman left her home and the husband called Ana Maria. He asked Ana Maria to talk to his wife. He shared that he had not hit her "that hard." Ana Maria stood firm and pointed out that his wife left him because she does not want to be beaten anymore. He struggled with understanding the difference between hitting her less and not hitting her at all. Ana Maria tried to explain to this husband that his wife is always bruised and is clearly being battered frequently. He did not seem to be embarrassed or ashamed of his behavior, and Ana Maria understood that her concerns were falling on deaf ears.

Ana Maria has been a child and youth advocate for years and is one of the cofounders of Panchita. Because these girls get yelled at constantly and frequently hear yelling all around them, the program has a "no yelling" rule. About 80 percent of the girls' mothers are domestic workers. Many of these women are migrants from Puno, Ayacucho, Cajamarca, or Sierra Sur. Most of the women speak Quechua—and one woman speaks only Quechua. Ana Maria conveyed that the women are very strong, and have seen such a horrifying level of violence that violence has become normalized for them, a remnant of the internal conflict. The result is that these mothers inflict violence on their daughters, too, which reveals why the Panchita childcare workshops are so important. Thus, one of the program's objectives is to improve the mother-daughter relationship. Ana Maria has noticed over the years that many of the girls have challenging relationships with their mothers, and yet this relationship is pivotal for them so the organization staff tries to improve it.

The stories of family violence are heart-wrenching. Ana Maria wondered how one actually stops the cycle of violence. She mentioned one story in which a girl was raped by her stepfather while her mother held her down. She said it is these kinds of egregious and nearly unthinkable forms of violence that render the situation hopeless. Again, it is hard for her and the team to not get involved, but they try to maintain boundaries for their own safety and well-being. Ana Maria has three trained psychologists as part of the team; together they work diligently to help these families heal and learn to nurture better and healthier family relationships free from violence.

Panchita visits the girls' homes during the week and sees the girls and their mothers on Saturdays. The girls, like their mothers, are filled with contradictions. Completing homework is not as encouraged as Ana Maria would like to see, though she understands that the terrible education leaves much to be desired. She said comments such as "It is so rare for her to do homework" are met by such responses from the father as "She must be sick." Panchita encourages these girls to complete their homework assignments, to further their education, even if it seems inadequate. Panchita tries to make three to six house visits during the week as a way to better understand the realities of the families that they work with in their program.

I remember returning to my rented apartment from this visit to the girls' program and wrestling with Ana Maria's comment—the feeling of hopelessness and needing to reach hundreds of girls to "save" a very small minority of them from a fate of exploitation and abuse. The burden of building a human rights culture is so laborious given such entrenched exploitation. And yet, we must begin somewhere, somehow. The program name—Support for the Future—underscores the human capital needed to create a different future. Panchita as a counterpublic navigates a present that is deeply haunted by its past, and works toward a future that is less hopeless despite that past.

Conclusion

I contend that the women leading the Panchita organization are part of a counterpublic seeking to forge ahead with human rights futures that consider the racial-gender legacy of exploitation in the employer–employee relationship and trying to nurture a future in which the tiers of citizenship are slowly eradicated. Seeking to undo centuries of racial, gender, and colonial logics wherein the dominant public has maintained such power is seriously challenging and thankless work. The mission and purpose of Panchita, from the workshops to the assistance with employment placement to the therapy sessions to creating programs for adolescent girls to creating a space for domestic workers of all ages to come together, is challenging the conditions of citizenship exclusion and social hierarchy.

The employer–domestic worker employee relationship resembles the power dynamic of white or mestizo elites and Indigenous noncitizens that existed during the Spanish conquest. The codependency that exists here in the realm of the home—wherein the elite engage in a practice of exploitation that is reliant on the subordination of the Indigenous noncitizen—means that the employer–domestic worker employee relationship is based in power. The exploitation of domestic workers is by no means new, nor is it unique to Perú. The incredible reliance on these domestic workers to care for the most personal of spaces—the home—produces a situation in which emotional abuse can become rampant and occurs out of public oversight.

The stigma associated with internally displaced people from certain regions can contribute to further marginalization, especially if they become domestic workers. In the case of forcible internal displacement in Perú stemming from the internal conflict starting in the 1980s, the stigma conditions the exploitation and abuse. The isolation that can accompany being of the forcibly displaced community produces a context in which pain and trauma become suppressed, producing new and difficult terrains for cultivating a human rights culture.

In this chapter I have situated the work of Panchita as related to human rights memory. Panchita is a labor rights defender for domestic workers as well as an advocate for girls' rights. In bringing these two areas together, Panchita is creating a counterpublic that grapples with the hardships and trauma inherited from the past (from the internal conflict and beyond) in the hopes of a new future. Through its programmatic work with adolescent girls, Panchita is tirelessly looking toward a future that is nonviolent and just.

In the final chapter, I discuss how in historically situating the emergence of human rights counterpublics, the haunting ghosts must be danced with in some way through the process of memory retrieval and dismantling tiers of citizenship. Acknowledging the history of trauma, of woundedness, will set forth new roots, a new foundation, for a Peruvian future in which the tiers of citizenship are undone through decolonial feminism and in which transformative memory can finally shine through.

CHAPTER 4

Ghosts, Hauntings, and Unsettling the Tiers of Citizenship

The 2021 presidential contest between Keiko Fujimori and Pedro Castillo symbolizes what is at stake for Perú—the future of the republic itself. When Fujimori lost the election to the political unknown Castillo, she loudly contested the results, making allegations of widespread fraud that had no basis in truth. Though Castillo's victory was by a razor-thin margin, Fujimori has come very close—too close—to winning the presidency three times. That she has come so close to attaining presidential power after what the country went through with her father, and when she stepped into the role of First Lady following her parents' estrangement, demonstrates that rampant support of her father has not declined. She is his channel, his offspring, in every sense of the word. Moreover, the Peruvian population has a penchant for authoritarianism in general, and therefore the production of transformative memory plays a determinative role in resisting those antidemocratic impulses.

Can Peruvian society, which has experienced decades of violence, shift from a context of rampant and widespread human rights violations to one of human rights realizations in the postconflict period? And is such a shift even possible when the conditions in which human rights abuses of the internal conflict flourished remain lurking after so many decades? The use of the word "transition" in "transitional justice" signals that a marked shift is taking place, symbolizing a break from the past. But the project of transitional justice is not so linear. Thus, moving toward the realization of human rights must be guided by transformative memory, a memory that reveals that society cannot go back to some preconflict past in which societal injustices were part of the status quo. The rebuilding of Peruvian society in the aftermath of the internal conflict must imagine a different Perú, one in which the tiers of citizenship are not embedded into every fabric of social life.

Scholars argue that it can take up to three decades to grapple with the ramifications of an internal conflict;[1] Perú is in its third postconflict decade. In comparison to other Latin American countries, Perú has been largely successful in its transitional justice efforts (e.g., the conviction of ex-president Alberto Fujimori for human rights violations, even though this verdict has been undermined, and the issuance of national apologies and a modest reparations program for those harmed during the internal conflict). However, scholars such as Rebecca Root argue that the achievements have been more symbolic than material.[2] Symbolic progress is important in that it can lead to material progress. On a fundamental level, for Dr. Salomón Lerner, a philosophy professor and chair of the Comisión de la Verdad y Reconciliación (CVR), the symbolic recognizes that the life of someone who has been deemed insignificant since the early formation of the Peruvian state is now viewed as valuable and important to the country's history and even its recovery.[3] For Lerner, symbolism is about morality and ethics as well as representation.

Anthropologist Kimberly Theidon's groundbreaking research on the violence from internal conflict in the Andean highlands of Ayacucho, a key site for this devastation, documents an intimate communal justice practice called *arrepentimiento* (repentance).[4] Though she found archival documents that suggest this practice pre-dates the internal conflict, *arrepentimiento* is a practice by which ex-Senderistas ask for forgiveness from their community peers, in which community members listening to the ex-Senderista must really *feel* their regret—meaning the repentant one must express genuine emotion when describing their actions in order to truly be forgiven by the community. In the conversations Theidon had with other Ayacuchans, this repentance process, when successful, results in a "tranquil heart," meaning that now villagers can live together again and move on from this terrible epoch of violence. She heard many insightful reasons why this outcome of a "tranquil heart" was far more desirable than enacting revenge, including that living with hate results in more harm, physically and psychologically.

As Theidon states, "Mass violence provokes a recalibration of perceptual and moral frameworks,"[5] underscoring how this context of unrelenting violence and repression forced people to make life decisions or choices based on this disorienting reality. Her point is a reminder that people's decisions or agency are shaped by their circumstances, and that we should not dismiss this context when people are caught between a horrendous choice and a terrible one. And so as Peruvian society continues in a different political moment in this transitional justice period, what is involved in this recalibration for the postmemory generation that has inherited the legacy of generational violence wherein their communities have been left with trauma, confusion, and pain? What can realigned perceptual and moral frameworks offer everyday Peruvians for having a dignified life?

Theidon further states, "The heart is the most important organ in terms of memory, health, and affliction and plays a central role in repentance and reconciliation."[6] Through the heart we are able to forgive and love, to feel emotions, to remember, and to remind ourselves of our human-ness, and even to feel present and strong in our physical bodies. Colonialism was such a violent enterprise of weakening the heart as much as possible, knowing that other aspects of life would be detrimentally affected. Through decolonial feminism, however, the heart can be the North Star, and thus, the starting point becomes healing the heart from trauma, honoring the various emotions that will emerge from that process rather than suppressing them, and protecting the health of the heart of the individual and the community.

In essence, this final chapter is about the heart and its relationships to transformative memory, focusing on two areas: (1) exploring the notion some Ayachucan villagers reported to Theidon that "too much memory" could actually do more harm, and (2) analyzing ten years of newspaper coverage from 2004 to 2013. The year 2013 marked the ten-year anniversary of the CVR report's public release. The CVR report remains the most seminal documentation of the Peruvian internal conflict, and therefore media coverage of that investigative work illuminates a public narrative about the internal conflict in the postconflict years. Discussion of the newspaper coverage includes highlighting select anniversaries, commemorations, and monuments; controversies and attacks against the CVR; and reports about the CVR's impact and legacy.

The chapter closes by explaining why human rights counterpublics provide a path toward reconciliation if society at large is open to this possibility and has a collective open heart. Human rights counterpublics provide new memory narratives and frameworks with which to understand the unspeakable and the traumas that stem from "unresolved social violence" that is structural and intimate. Reconciliation is not about a society without social conflict but rather about a society that can coexist in all its messiness and complexity as it is being guided by the heart. Refusing to engage in a transformative memory process will result in the perpetual existence of ghosts and hauntings for every generation, as unresolved social violence and conflict will not magically disappear. Put another way, how can the decolonial light appear in what seems like an impasse following the 2021 national elections?

Olvido: A Way Forward or Deafening Silence in the Case of Perú?

Why not just forget the violence of the internal conflict and move on? Importantly, how does "too much memory," as villagers reported to Theidon, actually do more harm, in which case reconciliation may never be possible? In such cases, forgetting is not a matter of convenience but rather of survival. Theidon states, "Forgetting is more than a strategy of the powerful over the weak. There are desired forgettings and, as Elizabeth Jelin has argued, 'There are forms of forgetting that are "necessary" for the survival and functioning of the individual subject as well as for groups and communities.'"[7]

The intimacy of the violence from the internal conflict, wherein for example villagers turned on one another, means that any kind of reconciliation has to include a deep rebuilding of community trust. This is not to say that Peruvians were trustworthy preconflict—quite frankly, everyone seems suspicious of everyone else, and the rampant government corruption feeds this mistrust. But any possibility of transformative memory emerging must directly engage with the profound distrust and suspicions Peruvians have of one another, because those sentiments are embedded in history too, and the internal conflict exacerbated them.

Political scientist Omar G. Encarnación discusses the politics of forgetting in the case of the Franco dictatorship in Spain. Addressing the role of what is known as the "Pacto de Olvido" (the Pact of Forgetting) in Spain, Encarnación argues that transitional justice does not have to abide by the same process of truth and reconciliation commissions, trials, and so forth to come out on the other side as a nation with a functioning democracy.[8] Yet, is there a cost to this silence in the case of Perú?

For Spain, oppositional parties opted to negotiate the "Pact of Forgetting," which was an "informal agreement [whereby] no one was put on trial for the political crimes of the old regime or disqualified from playing a role in the politics of the new democracy, since the pact was accompanied by a broad amnesty law that granted immunity for all political crimes committed prior to 1977."[9] This sweeping arrangement meant that there would be no truth commission, no official apology or condemnation of Franco's dictatorship regime, and that by and large, all elements typical of a transitional justice process would not apply here. Spain's democratic transition continued, and as Encarnación argues, that democratic outcome in Spain suggests that transitional justice methods and processes are not applicable for all national contexts and may in fact "become an obstacle to democratization."[10] He states that "there is no predestined outcome for democracy to the effort of holding an old regime accountable for its past misdeeds." And yet, Spain's colonial history situates it very differently than colonized countries like Perú, a country that inherited Spanish colonial racism, a legacy the country still embodies and that is the foundation to its anti-Indigenous ideology.

In addressing the structural and intimate forms of violence, Theidon further states, "There is a need to open space for 'positive forgetfulness' that liberates a person from an unbearable past. Forgetting and *remembering to forget* were leitmotifs throughout these communities."[11] "Positive forgetfulness" is an important dynamic to consider when confronting the tiers of citizenship in which forgetfulness can be misused as an instrument for and by the powerful. However, can some form of "positive forgetfulness" lead to a path of transformation or liberation too?

Positive forgetfulness should not be conflated with willful ignorance. And perhaps this distinction is what will provide communities the ability to determine to what extent forgetfulness is a viable method to engage, if at all. Therefore, who benefits from being forgetful: the affected community that has to figure out a way to live together again side by side, or those who made the decisions that exacerbated the violence and are then exempt from accountability? The decisions of elites, from the political to the military realms, are about the nation and how it represents and meets the needs of its citizens, especially the most vulnerable. In other words, the forms of forgiveness addressed by scholars like Theidon and Jelin are about the community, the village; that level of intimate forgiveness is not about *forgiving the nation* for its betrayal. And it is for this reason that forgiving the nation is less up for negotiation and why the work of the CVR report offers a starting point for that reconciliation journey based on its human rights documentation.

The CVR report is, in part, about the actions of individuals that changed the course of the nation's history; and now those in positions of decision-making power have the responsibility to heal the nation collectively from that historical trauma. To actually embark on that journey requires the activation of human rights memory. The media coverage discussed next provides insight into the shaping of the narrative about the internal conflict and the work of the CVR itself. Rather than create or contribute to an opening for human rights memory, the media coverage reveals an unwillingness to promote the results of the CVR, which would be an important starting point for Peruvian society at large.

Newspaper Media Coverage about the CVR and Its Final Report

For twenty-six months starting in 2001, the CVR undertook an extensive investigation, ultimately submitting its final report to the country in a ceremony in Ayacucho on August 28, 2003. The commission grew from seven to twelve representatives and added the term "reconciliation" to its title due to a revised mandate by former president Toledo. Though the commission's formation was met with some resistance, the breadth of the work is impressive. The CVR consisted of ten men and two women, with hundreds of support staff throughout the country.[12] Its methodology "included interviewing roughly 17,000 victims, holding public hearings and reconstructing hundreds of instances of atrocities through forensic and social research."[13] From this extensive investigation, the CVR "received testimonies that enabled [the commission] to identify by name 23,969 people who were either killed or disappeared during the internal armed conflict," with other statistical estimates indicating "that the number of victims in the conflict was 2.9 times greater than the recorded dead and disappeared," with the number "probably closer to 69,000."[14]

The newspaper coverage of the report reflects a type of memory in the making because it introduces a narrative about the internal conflict to the public; in this case the CVR was the most public and international symbol of a memory record about the internal conflict. This section discusses the narrative themes from the newspaper media coverage to delineate the messaging to the public regarding what happened in those two decades of 1980–2000. During the 2004–2012 period, two related themes become apparent in the newspaper coverage: (1) supporters of the CVR advocating for an enactment of the commission's recommendations, specifically on the fourth, eighth, and ninth anniversaries; and (2) the political right wing questioning the "legitimacy" of the CVR content, a challenge that extended to include subsequent controversies regarding the opening of a memory museum known today as El Lugar de la Memoria, la Tolerancia y la Inclusión Social (LUM). Once the CVR report became public, there was an opportunity to process its content, even beyond the borders of Perú, to determine the national memory (or memories) for a global audience. However, the report's very existence itself met with organized resistance right from the start.

More constructive public debate about how to achieve reconciliation was also the focus of newspaper coverage during this time, as well as the lack of government investment in fully realizing the CVR's recommendations for reparations, education, national apologies, and other memory work. The intent to foster a public debate without discrediting the CVR's work is especially vital for transformative memory. Contentious debates continue though, especially within Congress, alongside a conversation about restoration and repair based on newspaper coverage of the time period analyzed for this research.

The newspaper coverage regarding the heated disputes over the CVR had to do in part with its methodology and with how the commissioners classified victims. This critique or outrage corresponds to the debate about who deserves to be a victim. And herein lies a greater challenge when it comes to reconciliation. This dispute presumes that some set of criteria or personal deliberating body could make such a distinction. The Peruvian internal conflict is one in which that kind of binary ignores the fact that people, especially in Ayacucho, were sometimes caught between a bad choice and a worse one. When it comes to protecting your livelihood and your family, feeling enraged about being completely forgotten by the state can result in believing that there is no viable option but to respond with violence.

The backlash to the CVR always had been looming, and once substantial progress with regard to some of the more visible markers of memory such as LUM began, then the controversies came readily to the fore. The CVR was in support of creating a memory museum like the ones in Argentina, Chile, and South Africa, and to have it based in Lima, the epicenter of state power. However, the Peruvian government was not willing to fund its creation, and so the government of Germany offered to fund it. Although the García administration, which was then in power, initially rejected the idea, the Peruvian government ended up accepting the donation, and the construction of the museum began in 2012.

In addition, the challenges to opening LUM reveal that memory corresponding to state violence is always political, contested, and fraught, and results in the emergence of some difficult truths about corruption and abuse. A series of setbacks for LUM delayed its opening, including a steady rotation of directors. The current director, historian Manuel Burga, has been at the helm since August 2018.[15] When I was in Lima in 2015 hoping to visit this new museum, former LUM director Denise Ledgard had been fired. Realizing that I would not be able to visit LUM during this final research trip, I spoke to others, including Ledgard, about what else was going on. I learned about a tension that had divided many in the human rights community regarding LUM: whether or not to include *Yuyanapaq*, the curated collection of photos and other materials from the CVR that I had seen at the Museo Nacional. LUM's purpose became unclear: was it going to focus on a partial retrospective with *Yuyanapaq* as the centerpiece, and thus the endpoint, or would it reflect history alongside a longer period of time to chart a different future? Eventually this quandary was resolved and the plans for LUM proceeded without the inclusion of *Yuyanapaq*. For now the plan is to keep *Yuyanapaq* in the Museo Nacional until 2026, without much clarity yet as to where it will go after this date. Perhaps it will remain at the Museo Nacional.[16] In 2018 LUM hosted a fifteen-year retrospective in which *Yuyanapaq* was a temporary exhibit.[17] LUM officially opened its doors on December 17, 2015, about six months after I returned from my final research trip.[18]

CVR commissioners spoke to the media about the legitimacy of their work, defending its content, its methodology, and its record on the ten-year anniversary of the report's release. The growing resentment from conservative politicians such as Congressperson Martha Chávez, however, put human rights advocates and the commissioners in constant defense mode. Chávez even helped to dissolve a congressional human rights working group in 2013. First coming on the scene as a dedicated Fujimorista, Chávez has held a seat in Congress since 1995, and whenever possible has labored to stop any human rights memory work from taking shape.

Reviewing the newspaper coverage from 2004 to 2013 allows one to consider several key questions: What was the CVR's impact? And what is its legacy? How does the CVR become a living, breathing human rights document rather than being treated as the final chapter of a complicated book? How does a society move forward from such a national tragedy when the basis for what happened is heavily disputed, often further marginalizing those most directly affected by the conflict?

The public memory narrative documented in ten years of news media coverage as it relates to the work of the CVR reveals that the health of the (national) heart is fragile. The pedagogical triangle discussed in Chapter 2 stressed that head, heart, and ethics need to be simultaneously engaged in order to grow, to learn. In that first decade postconflict, opponents of the CVR's work kept their focus on trying to discredit their report. Upon realizing the CVR's report would have an influence over LUM's mission, they extended their criticism to LUM, delaying its opening for years by politicizing its existence. The determination by opponents to undermine the CVR, and by extension LUM, exists because they remain unwilling to recognize the trauma experienced by so many or they fundamentally lack empathy because they are also anti-Indigenous. And this form of racism is especially insidious to address because it is so vulgarly unethical to justify the targeting of people because of their region, their language (Quechua and Aymara), and their ethnicity or culture.

To rebuild society requires a recognition that society before was broken. And until that understanding is reached, at minimum, by those who remain opposed to memory production, then progress will be thwarted, preventing transformative memory from ever developing. Not coming to that minimal understanding underscores that the role of human rights counterpublics is to agitate for change, to create the opening in which transformative memory can be realized.

The Purpose of Human Rights Counterpublics

The purpose of counterpublics is to advance a counternarrative with which to challenge dominant or mainstream discourses about the internal conflict and its aftermath. Whether that be through art and storytelling or via policy proposals and advocacy, the counterpublic serves a distinct purpose in society. The counterpublic aspires to reach participatory democracy in which marginal voices no longer remain in the margins. How is the counterpublic trying to address past harms of communities who continue to be negated, ignored, or overlooked to the benefit of adversely affected communities?

The heterogeneity of counterpublic spheres—which range from the Indigenous to the subaltern to the virtual—demonstrates their vibrancy. In the case of Perú, Limeño human rights artists, such as those affiliated with Museo Itinerante Arte por la Memoria, are critical interlocutors because they practice a solidarity politics with subaltern groups, such as the Asociación Nacional de Familiares de Secuestrados, Detenidos y Desaparecidos del Perú (ANFASEP; National Association of Families of the Kidnapped, Detained and Disappeared of Perú). ANFASEP is an organization of families from Ayacucho who have been directly affected by the internal conflict and have connections to human rights organizations in Lima, such as the Asociación Pro Derechos Humanos and the Coordinadora Nacional de Derechos Humanos, to organize campaigns and events about the internal conflict.[19] ANFASEP also created its own memory museum in Ayacucho. ANFASEP can be described as a subaltern counterpublic for a number of reasons: its structure is organic and horizontal; its members are exclusively Andean- and Quechua-speaking mothers; during the internal conflict they and their families were direct targets of Sendero Luminoso and the state; and their communities experience extreme marginalization in Perú.

A serious engagement with counterpublics requires a willingness to acknowledge the ghosts and hauntings that remain ever present. In the next section, we consider what it would mean to move with the ghosts, to acknowledge their presence and hauntings but not be suffocated or even scared by them. Ghosts are forms of truths that do not want to be ignored. These are not truths to run away from or get defensive about. If we can move with the ghosts, then we can coexist with them in a way that can chart a future led by light instead of despair or distress or aggression.

One of the critiques I heard repeatedly from interviewees, and that is supported by other research, is that the CVR process depicted "victims" as poor, desolate, helpless (read: not knowing any better) people without any agency whatsoever. In other words, they had no choice: they were stuck between Sendero Luminoso and the military, and their being killed in massive numbers was in some ways unavoidable given the situation. This binary of perpetrator versus victim is a disservice to the context in which many communities were caught, between dreadful and sometimes coercive options, none of which fit neatly into this binary.

Humanities scholar Diana Taylor's work is useful in thinking about the urgency of counterpublics, meaning that it is through them that a new Peruvian identity can emerge postconflict that is not based on a Peruvian national identity rooted in anti-Indigenous sentiment, as Drinot argues. She writes:

> Doing one's nation-ness/gender "correctly" promises privilege and a sense of belonging, yet involves coercive mechanisms of identification. National/gender identity is not so much a question of being as of doing, of being seen doing, of identifying with the appropriate performative model. This identity is forged in the public sphere—the way we see others and ourselves is key to the process of a national recognition and identification. Identification is key to subject formation, though enactments vary from country to country and from period to period.[20]

The CVR was a process that could have initiated a national recognition with a public acknowledgment or reckoning of all the human rights violations from the internal conflict period. That process did not sufficiently happen, and thus a national recognition remains wholly incomplete.

Because El Ojo Que Llora contains the names of the people killed during the internal conflict or who are part of the disappeared, as well as the sites of major terror events during that period, such as the car bombing of Tarata Street and the targeting of leftist university students known as La Cantuta, the ghosts are being acknowledged, as is the haunting through the memorial's stone centerpiece, Pachamama. Or, as Avery Gordon puts it, "Of one thing I am sure: it's not that the ghosts don't exist."[21] As Mother Earth, Pachamama cries, and it is through the tears streaming down the centerpiece stone that the haunting is being reckoned with, because an emotional release is occurring. This same emotion is experienced by the visitor to this memorial site, because you can feel the ghosts staring at you through the names on the stones. The biographical dates and the years of disappearance that are etched into the stones are reminders that the dead are not being forgotten. This is a wholly different experience than being in a cemetery. The element that joins all of these lives is the haunting of social violence and the specter of racialized and patriarchal coloniality. And so if a new national identity can be forged in this public space, then perhaps, as Taylor argues, people can see themselves and each other through the formation of a new Peruvian national identity that is heterogenous and validates the trauma experienced during the internal conflict.

The point of reparation is to repair something damaged, to acknowledge a wrongdoing, and to make amends. In the United States, talk of reparations is often associated with slavery and viewed in terms of individual monetary compensation. This is not necessarily the case in Latin America. Activists in Perú have talked about economic reparations in terms of admissions quotas for colleges or as massive infusions of money and infrastructure for economically distressed communities. Any kind of reparations programs or reconciliation process must confront the ghosts that are sidelining justice. This also means that granting reparations to an individual, family, or community does not mean closure. Reparations in general are complicated and messy processes because a logic of neoliberal value is being imposed on a person killed or disappeared or on the family affected by the loss.

Following the release of the final CVR report in 2003, educators created curriculum units for use at elementary and high schools. But after right-wing pushback, that educational curriculum became too problematic for inclusion in the school, even in history books. This kind of exclusion is also an act of social violence—it willfully or intentionally keeps the younger generation from fully understanding the past. The artists and activists I spoke with talked about the importance of intergenerational dialogue when it comes to the internal conflict. This seems even more essential for the future leaders from the postmemory generation who need to avoid approaching politics ahistorically. How will this postmemory generation come to understand these ghosts and hauntings? Will the postmemory generation itself remain haunted if they don't learn about the CVR and the internal conflict?

In writing about Argentina's "Dirty War," Taylor states:

> The performativity of nation-ness involves a double mechanism—on one hand, nation-ness as the sum total of diverse "imaginings" is possible only because very different people imagine they share commonalities and learn to identify as part of a group. On the other hand, the hegemonic "nation" tends to suppress or appropriate diversity; otherness either disappears

or becomes absorbed as sameness. The Dirty War represents an extreme example of the double mechanism of imagining and imposition national/gender identity.[22]

In the case of Perú, the "share[d] commonalit[y]" was being unified in the state's fight against terrorist groups to save the republic; and yet, that imagining would only be possible by refusing to recognize the poverty and disenfranchisement the majority of Peruvians live in. Anyone perceived to be against this shared fight, whether real or perceived, was then a threat too. And second, recognizing that the Peruvians being impacted most significantly from the internal conflict did not speak Spanish, did not have literacy skills, and had been completely forgotten by the state meant that, regardless, they were deemed "foreign" or "othered" or "noncitizens" in their own country.

This chapter began with engaging the concept of *olvido* to discuss how the appropriateness of this practice depends on the community, but this concept is less applicable when working toward a national reconciliation, which needs to occur in Perú in order to build anew, to activate human rights memory, to recover and restore disjointed or disconnected communities, to put the hauntings to rest. Assessing ten years of newspaper coverage about the CVR reveals an incomplete public memory narrative emerging and one in which CVR commissioners expended effort in defending their work (and continue to do so), rather than explaining the outcomes of their investigation and offering a path forward. Unfortunately, then, the tiers of citizenship will remain the norm or the status quo in the media until the heart, coupled with the head and ethics, all come together in the community to foster memory production for social change.

Concluding Reflections

By centering the heart, everything shifts. Imagining a new Perú in which the ghosts rest and the hauntings dissipate seems like a utopian dream. And so, as I close this book, I return to this central organ, the heart, which controls everything: our mind, our feelings, our emotions, our futures. Centering the heart is not easy work, but without a focus on the heart, the memories recovered will be without meaning. The purpose of memory, and even of the CVR's report, is to confront certain societal truths, to reach transformative memory.

Formulating a counternarrative to the dominant public's narrative of Fujimori as savior must continue. The dominant Fujimori narrative is dangerous because it normalizes citizenship tiers, repression, and violence. This normalization ensures that divisions between residents, migrants, and refugees remain codified. These tiers are colonial scripts—they can be dismantled only by decolonial feminism, and only with heart. And so for this reason, the counterpublics discussed in this book—the political artists, the human rights activists, and the domestic worker advocates—are leading with heart. This heart work is deeply emotional and profoundly taxing. Yet without vibrant counterpublics in Perú, society is left with a gaping hole that invites authoritarianism. And so to restore, to rebuild, requires a rejection of colonial scripts meant to divide, a rejection of the myth of Fujimori as savior, and a full-throttled endorsement of participatory democracy and a rejection of corruption. The damage inflicted on El Ojo Que Llora and on the APRODEH mural discussed in Chapter 1, as well as other forms of backlash, mean that an unwillingness to move with the ghosts remains. In contrast, the passage of the Domestic Workers Law in June 2003, even though imperfect, benefits an overwhelmingly Andean community of women. This matters too when trying to make meaningful social change.

At the end of the day, the ghosts are going to keep haunting Peruvian society until they are confronted. And so, with heart, the work of Peruvian human rights counterpublics must continue. How societies respond to those difficult truths is what is at stake with the kinds of memories that come to the fore from those most adversely or directly affected. Are we open to hearing from them, or are their words too uncomfortable? As shown in Figure 4.1, we must activate human rights memory and take a nonlinear journey to reach transformative memory for lasting social change.

Is there hope? Maybe.

The Peruvian courts sentenced ex-president Alberto Fujimori to twenty-five years for human rights violations committed during his government's war against Sendero Luminoso in 2009. The fact is, though, that outstanding legal cases against Fujimori remain; therefore, his prison sentence does not in any way reflect the totality of the alleged wrongdoing during his dictatorship. Fujimori has never acknowledged guilt nor paid the millions he owes in "civil reparations." His actions and his ideological power over his political party will continue to haunt and complicate the production of human rights memory in Perú.[23]

Unfortunately, on March 17, 2022, in a 4–3 decision the Peruvian Constitutional Court reinstated the "humanitarian" pardon for ex-president Fujimori issued by Pedro Pablo Kuczynski in 2017.[24] It was overturned the following year, and Fujimori returned to prison, presumably to complete the remainder of his sentence, which will end on February 10, 2032.[25] He will be ninety-three years old by then. The reinstatement of the pardon was met with street protests by opponents of Fujimori, with those on social media using the hashtag #FujimoriNuncaMas. President Pedro Castillo appealed

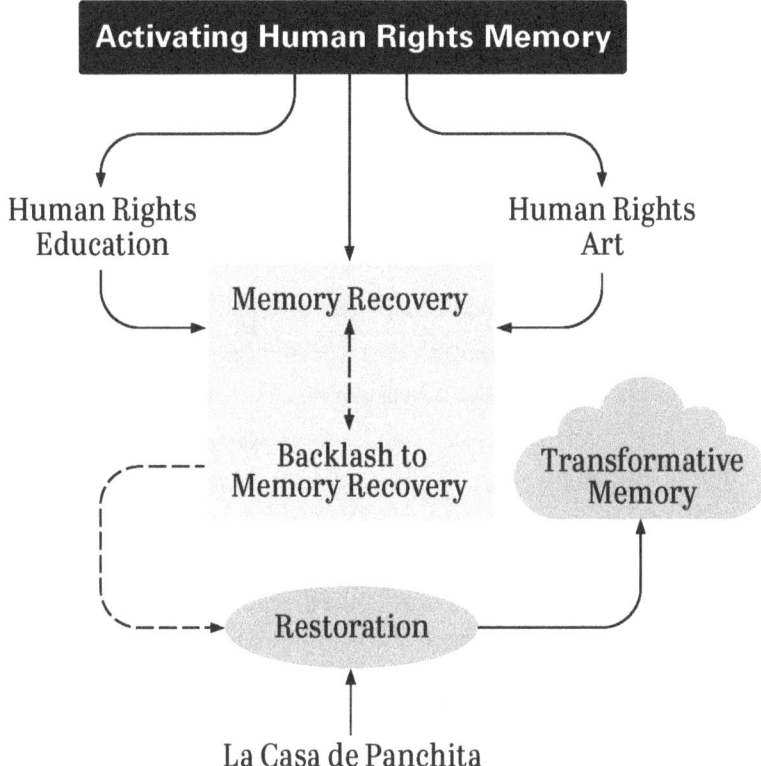

Figure 4.1. A flowchart depicting the path to transformative memory through a process for activating human rights memory by counterpublics involving education and art, which contribute to both the recovery of memory and backlash responses by the opposition.

to the Inter-American Court of Human Rights (IACHR) to intervene in this disastrous Peruvian court decision.²⁶ Court decisions that normalize impunity ensure that the wounds of Peruvian society remain open and that the trauma deepens. Even though the IACHR weighed in against Fujimori's release on April 8, 2022, Perú's constitutional court ordered Fujimori's release on humanitarian grounds on December 5, 2023. Prison officials released Fujimori the next day, and Keiko and her brother Kenji welcomed their father home. A difficult road and many challenges lie ahead and yet hope remains essential. As outraged as many people are about Fujimori's release, as well as Castillo's ouster and subsequent incarceration in December 2022, anger without hope is not the place from which transformative memory can happen.

Epilogue

By the end of 2019, the world was experiencing tremendous upheavals. In the Americas region, for example, there were ongoing uprisings in Bolivia, Chile, Brazil, Haiti, Perú, and the United States. In other parts of the world, uprisings in Hong Kong and Myanmar had garnered global attention as well. All of these uprisings were happening in the context of a global COVID-19 pandemic. And by 2020 the extent of the global pandemic meant that no one would be left unaffected.

The COVID-19 pandemic devastated Perú in comparison to the rest of the world, with mortality data analyzed by Johns Hopkins University indicating that proportionally in terms of its population size, Perú had the most COVID-19 deaths in the world.[1] I postponed planned trips in 2020, 2021, 2022, and 2023. In 2022 I was finishing another book in Spanish about the Peruvian feminist movement (*Voces de Mujeres Feministas Agentes de Cambio en Perú*) and thought it would be perfect timing to have a book launch in Lima in March 2023 and then finally go visit El Lugar de la Memoria, la Tolerancia y la Inclusión Social (LUM) in person (as mentioned in the Introduction, LUM had not officially opened during any of my research trips). Those hopes for an overdue return to Perú were dashed on December 7, 2022, when then-president Pedro Castillo attempted an ill-conceived coup in which he ended up being ousted and subsequently jailed. Perhaps Castillo felt he could repeat Fujimori's successful self-coup in April 1992. But with no political or military support, Castillo failed spectacularly.

And then the protests and repression started and continued at the time of writing this Epilogue, with calls for additional country-wide mobilization in July 2023. Those July 2023 protests were not as large-scale as the ones from previous months. The president who replaced Castillo is Dina Boluarte, the first woman president of Perú and Castillo's vice president, and she refuses to step down despite the people's demands that she resign. The protests had engulfed the entire country for part of 2023, from the north to the south, with the south being the most devastated. During this time, the violence unleashed by the government and its military resulted in over sixty people being killed, with thousands sustaining injuries. Amnesty International and Human Rights Watch released scathing reports in March and April 2023, respectively, resoundingly criticizing the government's repression and the slow pace and lack of transparency regarding investigations into civilian casualties.[2] Will anyone be held accountable for the civilian deaths and injuries from 2023?

A key demand from the street protests is a new election, to have a clean slate. President Boluarte initially seemed open to early elections, but talk of a new election has ended. Boluarte has the backing of the right-wing Congress and seems intent on remaining as president until the next scheduled elections in 2026. The protests have evolved over time since December 2022; at first they were about Castillo's ouster, and then they grew into protests about the deep social inequalities that pervade the country, disproportionately impacting Indigenous, Andean, Aymaran, and campesino communities.

The discourse of Fujimorismo, which had always been lingering especially with Keiko Fujimori remaining an active politician, was out in full force. The quickness with which this discourse surfaced in 2023 reveals that its reappearance was just a matter of time. Referring to the protesters as terrorists and rhetorically absolving the national police and the military of wrongdoing, President Boluarte has again normalized an anti-Indigenous discourse in which their dehumanization remains acceptable to the dominant public. As mentioned in Chapter 4, the ghosts are going to keep haunting Peruvian society because of the rationalizing, even justifying, of decades of violence targeting the most marginal in Peruvian society. The haunting is as clear as day in 2023.

On June 14, 2023, at a press conference in Piura, near the border of Ecuador, President Boluarte spoke out about the over sixty Peruvians who have been killed, explicitly blaming the protesters for their deaths. Clearly unsettled upon hearing that more protest mobilizations were planned for July to demand that she resign, Boluarte asked, "How many more deaths do they want? For the love of God! Doesn't it hurt their hearts to have lost over 60 people in these violent protests?"[3] She went on to say there had been no wrongdoing by the national police or the military and that the violence had not been instigated by the government.

In that same press conference, she also criticized community leaders who have spoken out against the violence, questioning how they have secured funding to travel internationally and then rhetorically asking whether their speaking out against Perú, especially outside of the country, should be considered an act of treason. She was most irritated with Verónika Mendoza, a left-wing politician from Cusco who has aspirations for national elected office and has been a presidential candidate in the past. This rhetoric of questioning their patriotism is to insinuate that they—Mendoza and other community leaders—are a threat to the country, like terrorists. On June 23, 2023, another massive protest took over the streets of Lima and Cusco in which the demands remained the same as for the past several months: new elections now!

We continue to live in precarious and dangerous times with emboldened global far-right conservative political parties blatantly engaged in power grabs. The political chaos since December 2022 is another wake-up call for Perú. And the coup attempt on January 6, 2021, in the United States is another wake-up call to the world that democracy can be destabilized anywhere, even in a global superpower nation. Elections have become spectacles and the peaceful transition of power is no longer to be taken for granted. The Republican Party has further embraced former president Trump since that horrific day of January 6, 2021, similar to how Fujimori supporters have encircled Fujimori.

So what does this politically toxic climate reveal about the possibility of transformative memory today? How can a human rights memory be activated in order to move the country to restore all its fragments? Unfortunately, the country is in a standoff and at a crossroads. Only time will tell if Perú picks the road to restoration. So many major events have happened in Perú since the conclusion of this research. The most obvious are the 2023 massive protests resulting from the failed self-coup attempt of President Castillo. In addition, former president Alan García committed suicide on April 17, 2019, as he was being arrested on corruption charges. Keiko Fujimori was in and out of prison (though released during the controversial 2021 national elections in which she refused to concede the election). Her father, Alberto Fujimori, was pardoned, then put back in prison, then released again, and then in April 2022 the IACHR intervened only to be released on humanitarian grounds in December 2023. This is a context in which the chaos feels never-ending. It's hard to imagine living through such daily turmoil and yet most of us in the world have chaos all around.

It is in this context of writing during chaos that I consider what Elizabeth Jelin states: "Dates and anniversaries are critical junctures in which memory is activated."[4] When this activation happens, new memories can also emerge.

Therefore, I explore this emergence by recognizing the transnational importance of provocative cultural intervention by Peruvian counterpublics, in the context of rising authoritarianism across the globe that portends renewed danger for those targeted by its fascist politics of white supremacy, xenophobia, and heteropatriarchy. In response, defenders of liberalism have critiqued the illiberalism of authoritarian populism. And yet, emerging from this schism between adherents of liberalism and those of authoritarianism is a powerful critique of both, a crack in the pavement where the light of a decolonial feminist imagination shines through. Liberalism is inadequate, as it leaves centuries-old structures of white supremacist settler-colonial capitalist patriarchy intact. As authoritarians attack the progressive reforms made possible globally by liberalism, and as liberal elites insist on liberal innocence, Peruvian women (Indigenous, African-descendants, and displaced) and human rights "artivists" (artists-activists) point us toward an emergent future that both vigorously contests authoritarian state power and refuses to exonerate liberalism from its implication in the social traumas from which Peruvians are struggling to liberate themselves. This decolonial praxis is emerging out of the failures of liberal transitional justice and through the reemergence of cosmologies that call on us to both embrace human rights and expand them to account for the dignity of all life that crosses multiple worlds (social, natural). It is in the decolonial praxis that transformative memory resides.

Latin American feminist philosopher Rita Segato argues, "It will be necessary to shake *the fantasy of the state, the fantasy of law* . . . sustaining the patriarchy and state certainties that impeded our advancement" as well as to reexamine "the unachievable, inclusive formula of human rights, 'different but equal,' which papers over the persistent, unassailable binary asymmetry in which a masculine subject who pretends to be universal prevails."[5] Segato is describing a legal approach to human rights that is the basis for much of the transitional justice efforts in Perú, an approach that will not provide the kind of opening or possibilities that societies need to build anew, as she correctly asserts. She is calling for a different type of political engagement, one that is rooted in the way women practice politics ("And politics will have to be feminine from now on"[6]). This engagement would necessitate human rights being viewed in a relational capacity, as culturally informed, and not bound to "the fantasy of the state, the fantasy of law."

Segato elaborates on the direction societies must take to abandon what has been broken. She states, "We need not only to *restore the ties of memory*—by looking in the mirror at our racialized image, an image inescapably anchored in our native landscape—but also to recover the value and reconnect to the memory of women's proscribed and devalued ways of practicing politics."[7] As she says, "The way forward in history will therefore involve affirming community and its bonds to rootedness," which will require "reconstituting the thread of memory."[8]

So what are those threads of memory in a place like Perú, where there are competing memories about what happened, some trying to invalidate others? This does not refer to those who want to willfully forget the past, as if the future were somehow detached from it. It refers instead to the intense debates occurring about the future of the country, the type of political leadership and elected representatives desired to steward the country, and how to actually change the social direction of the country in a way in which precarity is not the norm.

Toward a Politicized Human Rights Memory

Cultural interventions by Peruvian counterpublics are one method for achieving the transformative memory that is necessary for the rootedness that Segato calls for to take hold. This process of cultural intervention, however, is frustratingly slow and requires a willingness by society at large to seek such transformation. The Peruvian elections of 2021 and the ongoing uprisings of 2022 and 2023 have shown that the path leading to a different Perú remains deeply fraught, slow, and even twisted. The minefields of memory remain ever present: the tired tropes of activists and other street protesters being *terrucos*, or terrorists, and the inability to acknowledge the brutal attacks by the Peruvian police and military forces, which were devastating to many communities during and since the internal conflict, are wrong. "Minefields of memory" refers to the cultural or social "explosions" that occur every time the internal conflict comes up, whether at a family gathering or in the creation of a memory museum or in the latest social unrest. A minefield is an appropriate symbol in that you have to watch each and every step, tiptoeing even, to avoid setting off a backlash that would stymie memory work from happening at all.

Postconflict Perú now has memory museums in different parts of the country, of different sizes and with varying financial support. The multiple sites of memory signify that the purpose of memory varies, as the impact was felt differently throughout the country. At a virtual event hosted by LUM on May 29, 2021, called "Diálogo Reimaginar el LUM: Los museos de memoria en el Perú" (Dialogue Reimagining the LUM: Museums of Memory in Peru),[9] the coordinator from LUM, Enrique León, shared five of its guiding principles:

- Studying the history and memories of the period of violence from 1980 to 2000
- Reflecting on and learning from history and memories

- Building memories and knowledge
- Creating memories for life and instilling dignity
- Developing intertwined memory

The fourth and fifth items are especially relevant to transformative memory as they seek to acknowledge the potential of memory work in meeting the various realities of disparate communities. Creating memories for life and instilling dignity can be achieved if we appreciate that transformative memory is about rootedness, about culture, and about feminine politics, as argued by Segato. The artists, activists, and advocates discussed in this book are seeking to establish a new foundation for Perú by engaging with memory for life and with dignity in different capacities and by drawing from various cosmologies.

Cynthia Milton's work is particularly insightful for navigating this memory terrain, as she writes about both memory knots and conflicted memories. For Milton, the defacing of public memory murals such as El Ojo Que Llora signifies a major cultural clash about whose memories—and with them, whose pain and trauma—matter. This cultural collision is portrayed largely among the citizenry, but what about the military, which also engages in its own form of memory making that may "not necessarily [be] false or fabricated, but contorted"?[10] For Milton, this somewhat overlooked constituency in terms of memory production—the Peruvian military—is also somewhat divided on the internal conflict. Yet the Peruvian military has a shared objective in questioning the Comisión de la Verdad y Reconciliación (CVR) report, which described the military as culpable of egregious wrongdoing and abuse.

As much as military officers are trying to advance different narratives about the internal conflict, as researched by Milton, memory studies are not a form of nostalgia about a joyous precolonial past but rather an attempt to create a politicized human rights memory for the present and the future. A singular portrayal of memory about the internal conflict and its antecedents would risk the reproduction of a universal memory narrative like the universal masculine subject, while memory recovery efforts that provide new outlooks on the present and the future could ultimately be transformative in terms of moving the dialogue away from stagnation and regression.

José Carlos Agüero wrote a poignant, poetic memoir about being the son of Shining Path members that has now been translated into English by Latin American studies professors Michael Lazzara and Charles Walker. One of the emotions that Agüero returns to throughout the memoir is that of guilt; he even has a chapter titled "Guilt." This was the guilt he felt knowing that his parents had severely harmed people with their militancy, or guilt that as an urban youth he himself had been involved in some of the transactions advancing the Shining Path's cause. As Agüero wrestles with this understandable feeling, he also provokes a question about the interrelationship between guilt and transformative memory.

Agüero's memoir points out that the human emotion of guilt might be a major barrier to doing memory work in Perú. His point resonates given that the binary of victim and perpetrator is not useful and that guilt itself is multilayered—whether you are the son of terrorists, as Agüero is; a police or military officer haunted by the violence performed by your hands; a neighbor who betrayed another neighbor to save your own life; or the survivor of an atrocity (i.e., survivor's guilt). All of these forms of guilt can create paralysis when it comes to memory work, making the process of transformative memory profoundly painful. As Agüero states:

> We might want to think about the forces that shaped, conditioned, and influenced people's decisions, or that made it difficult if not impossible for them to make those decisions, or that plunged them into the dilemma of having to make decisions where costs—moral, economic, political, or simply human—were extreme. We're already familiar with some of those costs: having to decide to kill neighbors, family members, or Shining Path militants to prove their loyalty to the armed forces. In my case, that was agency—a miserable kind of agency.[11]

And herein is the truth: what good is agency if your only exercise of it is miserable?

Agüero makes an important delineation between a Senderista, a person, and the Shining Path, the institution. He states, "Every Senderista had his or her way of being in Sendero, and all Senderistas existed in tension with the institution that was the Shining Path."[12] Many institutions seek to control people, and therefore, the institution can be denounced in a way that does not have to demonize the person. Institutions do not protect everyday people.

The English version of Agüero's memoir closes with an interview he did with the editors, Lazzara and Walker. Agüero's poignant closing remarks in that interview attempt to chart a direction for those willing to cultivate a human rights memory:

> To move forward, though, we have to accept the reality that we are living in a post conflict country: that there are crimes we still must acknowledge, that there are actions or omissions to which we still must admit, and that one of our first tasks as a society must be to create the institutional and societal conditions in which we can talk about difficult subjects without

taboo. If we can't do that, reconciliation won't ever be viable. Yet it's still a worthwhile process that we need to set in motion if we ever hope to live just a little bit better.[13]

Agüero states that the conditions must be present, both institutionally and socially, in which to openly dialogue about issues that will make people uncomfortable. It is in these spaces of discomfort that reconciliation and restoration can occur. To emerge anew as a society, with a true recognition for the dignity of all life (human and nonhuman), would mean choosing the path with heart.

This is in part why the work of Panchita is so important, as the organization is a critical interlocutor in an employer-employee relationship that has long been fraught with exploitation. In that capacity, the women of Panchita are disruptors of a colonial legacy in which elites have an incredible amount of power over Indigenous peoples. These power dynamics are present when a domestic worker has been displaced and forced to migrate to Lima; they are present when an employer sexually and/or racially harasses a domestic worker; and they are present when an employer forbids time off for domestic workers. Engaging in this process of contract negotiation together is a form of acknowledging that past power dynamics, which thrived on exploitation, can no longer continue. And Panchita's workshops are a way to underscore that knowledge is power.

Talking about the internal conflict "without taboo" is the only way to reach transformative memory. Participating in the Memory Game and going to sites such as LUM and El Ojo Que Llora are ideal contexts in which to reflect, listen, and learn. And yet the latter two, LUM and El Ojo Que Llora, have been met with controversies, as people who are hostile to their symbolism or purpose challenge their very existence. But in 2018 LUM finally opened, thanks to funds from the government of Germany, and on January 21, 2022, the Peruvian government designated the memorial El Ojo Que Llora a national cultural heritage site.[14] These are glimmers of light in a sea of darkness.

The postmemory literature helped me realize that I am part of a postmemory generation that lives in the diaspora, and that I too was learning about the internal conflict, not exclusively from my immediate family members per se but from scholarship and from reading Peruvian newspapers. I realized I was on some level searching for my own memory, because the reality is that if my parents had not migrated, I would have lived in Lima. Perhaps that is why engaging in research about memory in Perú feels both oddly personal and distant for me. I continue to reside in that liminal space not only as an individual person but also as a member of a transnational Peruvian family living in the US empire.

We also continue to live through a COVID-19 pandemic from which the global aftershocks will continue for generations. The research conducted for this book happened at a completely different time; in fact, it feels like an entirely different lifetime. A global pandemic should in fact make matters crystal clear: our fates and destinies are interconnected. As the COVID-19 vaccine rolled out, some in the United States quickly got vaccinated, hoping that their lives would resume to normalcy. But if that normalcy involved international travel, whether for pleasure or to see family and friends, they were in for a rude awakening. I had always imagined one final trip to Perú to visit LUM in person. But with the political climate, the freezing of funds, revolving directors, and delayed openings, and then the start of the pandemic, I never got my chance. And so, like so many other researchers, I had to rely on the virtual and digital space to engage with LUM's work.[15] Opponents of LUM remain active: the right-wing conservative mayor of Lima, Rafael López Aliaga, forced the closure of LUM temporarily in April 2023 claiming safety code violations. López has always been an opponent of LUM, asserting the museum advanced a false narrative about the role of the military in the internal conflict, specifically that the military was culpable of wrongdoing.[16] LUM has since reopened.

Agüero wrote a compelling op-ed in the *Washington Post* on March 7, 2023, about the ongoing Peruvian crisis, stating:

> The country is currently at an impasse. But regardless of its final outcome, the crisis is likely to end up becoming a pivotal moment in the reimagining of Peruvian citizenship, and Peruvian democracy. In Peru, there are people aged 70 or 80, who have lived their entire lives under the quasi-feudal servitude of large estates, or gamonales. Not being able to read, they were denied the right to vote until 1980. They have faced violence and repression when fighting for land rights. They have survived hyperinflation, a cholera epidemic, terrorism, dictatorship, racism, hunger, at least two transitions to democracy, a poorly handled pandemic that killed about 220,000 people.[17]

Noting the perpetual state of political crisis with six presidents in six years, Agüero clarifies what is at stake, especially for the people protesting who "are from the regions with the highest poverty levels" and have been targeted by Fujimoristas to void their votes. As he states, "They, more than anyone, are fighting to retain the last shred of democracy they still have left."

Even though I was born and live in the United States, I understand that I am part of a global community, which is why the turmoil in Perú pains me as much as the turmoil in the United States. The COVID-19 pandemic has shown in the most devastating way the fragility of the human race, the toxic nature of disinformation, and the real dangers of authoritarians and dictators and their supporters. To say that the world has broken my heart dozens of times since writing this book would be an understatement. A global reckoning is also occurring at a magnitude previously unseen, in which Perú as a society must delve deeply into interrogating its entrenched anti-Indian past to determine its decolonial future and to come out on the other side a humane, just, and hopeful place.

Notes

Preface

1. Portions of these remarks were first shared at a March 2, 2022 UC Santa Cruz event titled "Solidarities for Justice" celebrating the naming of John R. Lewis College on campus.

Introduction

1. BBC Mundo. "El 'símbolo' de Panchita."
2. Bueno-Hansen, *Feminist and Human Rights Struggles in Peru*.
3. Farell and Seipp, *The Road to Peace*, 13.
4. Ibid.
5. Drinot, *The Allure of Labor*.
6. Comisión de la Verdad y Reconciliación, "Informe Final," 2003.
7. Li, *Unearthing Conflict*.
8. Root, *Transitional Justice in Peru*, 8.
9. Ibid.
10. Degregori, *How Difficult It Is to Be God*, 182.
11. Teitel, "Transitional Justice Genealogy," 69.
12. Zarate and Casey, "Fujimori Is Ordered back to Prison in Peru, Angering Supporters."
13. Milton, ed., *Art from a Fractured Past*, 9.
14. Ibid., 10.
15. See Abrego, *Sacrificing Families*.
16. Amnesty International, *Annual Report: Peru 2010*, May 28, 2010.
17. Farell and Seipp, *The Road to Peace*, 11.
18. Bueno-Hansen, *Feminist and Human Rights Struggles*.
19. Ibid., 13–14.

20. Ibid., 15.
21. Li, *Unearthing Conflict*.
22. Lust, "Social Struggle and the Political Economy of Natural Resource Extraction in Peru."
23. Ibid., 196.
24. Root, *Transitional Justice in Peru*, 162.
25. See Degregori, *How Difficult It Is to Be God*.
26. Li, *Unearthing Conflict*.
27. "The two candidates were separated by just 44,000 votes out of nearly 19 million cast." Simeon Tegel, "Pedro Castillo Finally Declared Winner of Peru's Presidential Election."
28. Ong, "Powers of Sovereignty," 24–35; Scott, *Seeing Like a State*; and Pitarch, Speed, and Solano, eds., *Human Rights in the Maya Region*.
29. Fraser, "Rethinking the Public Sphere," 56–80.
30. Felski, *Beyond Feminist Aesthetics*, 166.
31. Loehwing and Motter, "Publics, Counterpublics, and the Promise of Democracy," 227.
32. Degregori, *How Difficult It Is to Be God*, 181.
33. *La Republica*, "Solo 34% de peruanos conoce la comisión que investigó violencia terrorista."
34. Ramírez et al., eds., *Precarity and Belonging*.
35. Migrants, regardless of status, are considered noncitizens.
36. Drinot, *Allure of Labor*, 15.
37. Ibid.
38. Bueno-Hansen, *Feminist and Human Rights Struggles*.
39. See the Quipu Project: https://interactive.quipu-project.com/#/en/quipu/intro.
40. Bueno-Hansen, *Feminist and Human Rights Struggles*.
41. This point comes from a commentary offered by Angela Davis in the documentary *13th* (film by Ava DuVernay) about the problem with criminal justice reform.
42. Falcón, *Power Interrupted*.
43. Enloe, *The Curious Feminist*.
44. Burt, "Accounting for Murder."
45. Dr. Salomón Lerner delivered these remarks in Spanish at Brandeis University on December 1, 2011, at an event called "Just Performance: Enacting Justice in the Wake of Violence."
46. All of this qualitative data was analyzed using the software program NVivo. I coded and analyzed interview transcripts, field notes, newspaper coverage, online research, and photos. Through thematic coding followed by memo writing, I analyzed the collected data extensively and thoroughly; the findings of this analysis are shared in this book.
47. CVR Press Release 226, "TRC Final Report was made public on August 28th 2003 at noon."

Chapter 1. Backlash to Building Human Rights Memory

1. Jorge Miyuigi, interview with the author, June 27, 2013, in Lima, Perú.
2. Drinot, *The Allure of Labor*.
3. Mauricio Delgado Castillo, interview with the author, July 1, 2013, in Lima, Perú.
4. "Hatun Willakuy: Abbreviated Version of the Peruvian Final Report of the Truth and Reconciliation Commission."
5. See Milton, "Curating Memories of Armed State Actors in Peru's Era of Transitional Justice," 361–78.
6. Lehrer and Milton, "Introduction: Witnesses to Witnessing," 6–7 n.14.
7. Jelin, "Silences, Visibility, and Agency," 188 n.22.
8. Select sections in this chapter first appeared in Falcón, "Intersectionality and the Arts," used here with permission.
9. La Serna, *Corner of the Living*, 1.
10. Ibid.
11. Degregori, *How Difficult It Is to Be God*; La Serna, *Corner of the Living*.
12. La Serna, *Corner of the Living*, 1. See also Theidon, *Intimate Enemies*.
13. Hatun Willakuy, 84–85. See also DeGregori, *How Difficult It Is to Be God*, 24 n.6.
14. Starn, "Maoism in the Andes," 399–421.
15. Historian Robin Kirk wrote the following about the three men: "They were the three who had voluntarily presented themselves in court after being summoned. None spoke Spanish. No interpreter was provided. The men were convicted. In prison, Simeón Aucatoma, seventy, succumbed to tuberculosis. Dionisio Morales, who maintained that he had been in Iquicha that day, served his time and then dropped from view." Kirk added that Manuel Ccasani served seven years and was living at the time in a refugee camp with his family and did not want to talk about the reporters. Kirk, *The Monkey's Paw*, 200.
16. Degregori, *How Difficult It Is to Be God*, 106.
17. Heiberg, O'Leary, and Tirman, eds., *Terror, Insurgency, and the State*, 318.
18. Starn, "Maoism in the Andes," 405.
19. Ibid., 406.
20. Ibid., 406–11.
21. Ibid., 409.
22. Ibid., 399.
23. Ibid., 412, as quoted by Antonio Diaz Martinez in Jose Maria Salcedo, 'Con Sendero en Lurigancho', *Quehacer*, no. 39 (1986), p. 62.
24. Ibid., 414.
25. Ibid., 416.
26. Burt, "Accounting for Murder."
27. Perry, producer and director, *The Fall of Fujimori*.
28. Mauceri, "State Reform, Coalitions, and the Neoliberal Autogolpe," 8.
29. Ibid., 9.

30. See Klein, *Shock Doctrine*.
31. This book does not discuss the MRTA in depth, but Fujimori destroyed this smaller guerrilla group after a four-month-long hostage crisis at the Japanese embassy in Lima. For more about the Túpac Amaru namesake, see Walker, *The Tupac Amaru Rebellion*.
32. Hancock, "When Multiplication Doesn't Equal Quick Addition," 74.
33. Ibid., 67.
34. Falcón, "Transnational Feminism and Contextualized Intersectionality at the 2001 World Conference against Racism," 101.
35. Falcón, *Power Interrupted*.
36. Mantilla Falcón, "Gender and Human Rights," 129–42.
37. Stephenson, "Forging an Indigenous Counterpublic Sphere," 101.
38. Gómez-Barris, *Where Memory Dwells*, 5.
39. Jelin, "Silences, Visibility and Agency." See also Jelin, "Silences, Visibility, and Agency," in *Identities in Transition*, 187–213.
40. Fraser, "Rethinking the Public Sphere," 56–80.
41. Felski, *Beyond Feminist Aesthetics*, 166.
42. Hancock, *Intersectionality*; Cho, Crenshaw, and McCall, "Toward a Field of Intersectionality," 785–810; Choo and Ferree, "Practicing Intersectionality in Sociological Research," 129–49.
43. Delfín, "Inside the Artist's Studio."
44. For more images of Delfín's work, see Delfín, "Inside the Artist's Studio."
45. Ibid., 19 n.1.
46. Ibid.
47. APRODEH, "Visión," accessed January 29, 2024, https://www.aprodeh.org.pe/visionmision/ (author's translation).
48. Delfín, "Inside the Artist's Studio," 227 n.1.
49. *La República*, "El ojo que llora."
50. Theidon, *Intimate Enemies*.
51. Planas, "Lika Mutal murió."
52. Vargas Llosa, "El ojo que llora."
53. Hite, "'The Eye That Cries,'" 108–34. See also Milton, "Defacing Memory," 161–78.
54. Hite, "'The Eye That Cries,'" 121–22 n.32.
55. Romero, "As Ex-President Faces Trial, a Reckoning for Peru."
56. See Theidon, *Intimate Enemies*.
57. Drinot, *Allure of Labor*, 23 n.36. See also Saona, *Memory Matters in Transitional Peru*.
58. Saona, *Memory Matters in Transitional Peru*, 88 n.39.
59. Hite, "'The Eye That Cries,'" 128. See also Theidon, *Intimate Enemies*, 38.
60. Bacchetta et al., "Transnational Feminist Practices against War," 305.
61. Jelin, "Silences, Visibility, and Agency," 210 n.22.
62. Saona, *Memory Matters in Transitional Peru*, 89 n.39.
63. Milton, "Defacing Memory," 2 n.3.

Chapter 2. Memory Recovery through Art and Education

1. *La República*, "Yuyachkani presenta: Sin Título técnica mixta—Revisado." In Spanish, the quote about Sin Tutolo states, "[Una] gran instala-acción escénica en las fronteras del teatro documento, las artes visuales y la performance, donde actores y espectadores comparten el mismo espacio, el cual sugiere el desván de un museo de historia donde convergen documentación, imágenes y elementos de dos períodos de la historia peruana, la Guerra del Pacífico (Siglo XIX) y el conflicto armado interno (Siglo XX)."

2. Select sections in this chapter first appeared in Falcón, "Intersectionality and the Arts," used here with permission.

3. La Coordinadora Nacional de Derechos Humanos @cnddhhperu, Instagram post, January 24, 2022, https://www.instagram.com/p/CZIlpRylXUL/.

4. Milton, *Conflicted Memory*, 3.

5. Ibid.

6. Facing History, "Responding to the Insurrection at the U.S. Capitol."

7. Vargas Llosa, "El ojo que llora." Vargas Llosa is a controversial author known for making problematic remarks about Indigenous communities and women.

8. Sonia was very clear that the gathering should not be referred to as a "funeral" but rather a "gathering" or "commemoration." Javier's body has not been found, and until that happens, he remains alive in some way for her family.

9. Alexander, *Pedagogies of Crossing*, 289.

10. Ibid., 326.

11. Lugones, "Toward a Decolonial Feminism," 742–59.

12. Dosek and Parendes, "Peru Might Elect an Authoritarian President."

13. Carrión, *The Fujimori Legacy*.

14. Statista, "Level of Education of the Population Aged 25 and Older in Peru in 2017, by Area of Residence."

15. Castañeda, "Análisis del discurso de la canción 'Flor de Retama'" thesis, 2. See also Vich, *Poéticas de duelo*, 23.

16. Milton, ed., *Art from a Fractured Past*, 76.

17. The limitation of this research is that it discusses only art projects based in Lima or by Lima-based artists; examining transitional justice art projects produced outside of Lima would enhance this research.

18. They first shot María Elena Moyano dead and then placed bombs under her body. All of this occurred in front of her two young sons.

19. Jorge Miyuigi, interview with the author, June 27, 2013, in Lima, Perú.

20. The quotes in the following paragraphs come from a photo I took of the sign at the Museo Itinerante exhibit. The translations are my own.

21. The entire poster series is part of an independent art project by Mauricio Delgado Castillo that can be seen at Un Día en la Memoria, www.undiaenlamemoria.blogspot.com (accessed October 25, 2017). This specific poster was seen during my visit to the Museo Itinerante exhibit in Lima.

22. Mauricio Delgado Castillo @mauriciodelgadlocastillo, Instagram post, March 13, 2022, https://www.instagram.com/p/CbD3PM1OaCE/.

23. Some of their stories are available at The Quipu Project, https://interactive.quipu-project.com/#/en/quipu/intro (accessed October 16, 2017).

24. Ewig, "Hijacking Global Feminism," 632–59.

Chapter 3. *No Somos Invisibles*

1. Gordon, *Ghostly Matters*.

2. See Superintendencia Nacional de Fiscalización Laboral, "Nueva Ley de Trabajadoras y Trabajadores del Hogar"; Salazar, "Reglamento de la ley de trabajadoras del hogar entra en vigencia desde hoy"; and Colchado, "Nueva ley de trabajadoras del hogar: estos son los cambios aprobados."

3. Blofield, *Care Work and Class*, 10. The other forms of domestic work, such as gardening, occur outside of the private home sphere.

4. Stepputat and Sørensen, "IDPs and Mobile Livelihoods."

5. Ibid.

6. Bunster and Chaney, *Sellers and Servants*, 17–22.

7. Blofield, *Care Work and Class*, 44.

8. See Blofield, *Care Work and Class*.

9. Gordon, *Ghostly Matters*, 4.

10. Ibid.; emphasis mine.

11. Ibid., xvi.

12. Drinot, *The Allure of Labor*.

13. Ibid., 13.

14. Ibid., 15.

15. Burt, *Political Violence and the Authoritarian State in Peru*.

16. Gordon, *Ghostly Matters*, 18.

17. See the Quipu Project, in which you can hear directly from women affected by forcible sterilization, at https://interactive.quipu-project.com/#/en/quipu/intro.

18. Gutiérrez-Rodríguez, *Migration, Domestic Work, and Affect*, 5.

19. Blofield, *Care Work and Class*, 29. Blofield notes that there is uncertainty with regard to the hours. She states, "In Peru, 48 hours explicitly applies only to live-in domestic workers, although the Ministry of Labor has interpreted it to apply to all domestic workers." See also ibid., 44–45.

20. Ibid., 70. Blofield credits Alejandro M. Estévez and Susana C. Esper for the term "chronic informality." See Estévez and Esper, "La relación entre el Sistema impositivo y la desigualdad."

21. Cherríe Moraga, interview by Kelly Anderson.

22. This currency conversion is based on an exchange rate of S/.2.8 per US$1 at the time of this research.

23. Hilgers, "Out of the Shadows."

24. I was able to observe only the first half of this workshop.

25. Sofia, the Panchita staff person and workshop cofacilitator, told me that a prior session had had thirteen participants.

26. Note this is during the time of my research and so the wage has likely increased by now.

27. Ana Maria also works in a district called Nueva Rinconada, which is a very poor area in the Lima outskirts.

Chapter 4. Ghosts, Hauntings, and Unsettling the Tiers of Citizenship

1. Weld, *Paper Cadavers*.
2. Root, *Transitional Justice in Peru*.
3. Dr. Salomón Lerner, interview with the author, August 12, 2015, in Lima, Perú.
4. Theidon, *Intimate Enemies*, 50.
5. Ibid., 15.
6. Ibid., 48.
7. Ibid., 42.
8. Encarnación, *Democracy Without Justice in Spain*.
9. Ibid., 1–2.
10. Ibid., 188.
11. Theidon, *Intimate Enemies*, 42.
12. Heilman, "Truth and Reconciliation Commission of Peru."
13. "Hatun Willakuy: Abbreviated Version of the Final Report of the Truth and Reconciliation Commission."
14. See ibid., 12. The report notes, "Using a methodology known as Multiple Systems Estimation, the CVR calculates that the number of Peruvians killed or disappeared in the internal armed conflict was probably closer to 69,000." As cited in the footnote, "The calculation of 69,280 victims has a 95-percent accuracy rate, with the lower calculation at 61,007 victims and the higher calculation 77,552 victims."
15. Canal N, "Manuel Burga Díaz fue designado director del LUM."
16. See "Yuyanapaq," Art and Reconciliation: Conflict, Culture and Community, accessed July 16, 2022, https://artreconciliation.org/arts-and-reconciliation/case-studies/yuyanapaq/.
17. LUM press release, "Para recordar Yuyanapaq: 15 años después."
18. Feldman, *Memories before the State*, vii.
19. To learn more about ANFASEP, see http://anfasep.org.pe/.
20. Taylor, *Disappearing Acts*, 92.
21. Gordon, *Ghostly Matters*, 12.
22. Taylor, *Disappearing Acts*, 92–93.
23. Taj, "Peru's Top Court."
24. Ibid. As stated in the article, one of the justices died in 2021, and this justice was against freeing Fujimori.
25. Associated Press, "Peru Court Orders Ex-President Fujimori Freed from Prison."

26. Pedro Castillo Terrones @PedroCastilloTe, Twitter post, March 17, 2022, https://twitter.com/PedroCastilloTe/status/1504556634634616832?s=20&t=lJL QuMsPB60qyysi3I7qqg.

27. Rochabrun, "Inter-American Court Orders Peru Not to Release Fujimori from Prison."

Epilogue

1. Beaubien, "Peru Has the World's Highest COVID Death Rate. Here's Why"; Johns Hopkins University and Medicine, Coronavirus Resource Center, "Mortality in the most affected countries."

2. Amnesty International, "Peru"; Human Rights Watch, "Deadly Decline."

3. The entire press conference can be seen on TV Perú Noticias, which is a state-funded news outlet. She begins discussing the protesters at the 2:25 mark. In Spanish, President Boluarte said, "¿Cuántas muertes más quieren? ¡Por amor de Dios! Acaso no les duele en el alma haber perdido más de 60 personas en esas movilizaciones violentas." See TV Perú Noticias, "Presidente Dina Boluarte en Piura, hoy martes 14 de junio del 2023."

4. Jelin, "The Minefields of Memory."

5. Segato, "A Manifesto in Four Themes," 205.

6. Ibid., 210.

7. Ibid., 207; emphasis mine.

8. Ibid., 210.

9. "Diálogo Reimaginar el LUM: Los museos de memoria en el Perú," LUM webinar, YouTube, May 29, 2021, https://www.youtube.com/watch?v=4gl9 DSYaHXA.

10. Milton, *Conflicted Memory*, 3.

11. Agüero, *The Surrendered*, 82.

12. Ibid., 52.

13. Ibid., 129.

14. The Peruvian government resolution for declaring El Ojo Que Llora as an official cultural site is "Declaran Patrimonio Cultural de la Nación al memorial 'El Ojo que Llora' de propiedad de la Asociación Civil Caminos de la Memoria." *El Peruano*.

15. Many of the webinars hosted by LUM make it to their YouTube page, available at https://www.youtube.com/channel/UC6TpI7VrAq5s71T79kUF3wA.

16. Collyns, "Mayor Closes Museum of Memories in Battle over Story of Peru's Violent Past."

17. Agüero, "Why Peru's Crisis Is Worth Studying Closely by Democracies Everywhere."

Bibliography

Abrego, Leisy J. *Sacrificing Families: Navigating Laws, Labor, and Love across Borders.* Palo Alto, CA: Stanford University Press, 2014.
Agüero, José Carlos. *The Surrendered: Reflections by a Son of Shining Path.* Edited and translated by Michael J. Lazzara and Charles F. Walker. Durham, NC: Duke University Press, 2021.
———. "Why Peru's Crisis Is Worth Studying Closely by Democracies Everywhere," *Washington Post*, March 7, 2023, https://www.washingtonpost.com/opinions/2023/03/07/peru-protests-democracy-economy/.
Alexander, M. Jacqui. *Pedagogies of Crossing: Meditations on Feminism, Sexual Politics, Memory, and the Sacred.* Durham, NC: Duke University Press, 2006.
Amnesty International. "Peru: Racist repression and slow investigation continue 100 days after protests began," March 16, 2023, https://www.amnesty.org/en/latest/news/2023/03/peru-racist-repression-slow-investigations-100-days/.
———. Annual Report: Peru 2010, May 28, 2010, https://www.amnestyusa.org/reports/annual-report-peru-2010/3/.
Asociación Pro Derechos Humanos (APRODEH). "Misión." APRODEH.org, accessed February 5, 2024, https://www.aprodeh.org.pe/visionmision/.
Associated Press. "Peru Court Orders Ex-President Fujimori Freed from Prison," *National Public Radio (NPR)*, March 18, 2022, https://www.npr.org/2022/03/18/1087442224/peru-court-orders-ex-president-fujimori-freed-from-prison.
Bacchetta, Paola, Tina Campt, Inderpal Grewal, Caren Kaplan, Minoo Moallem, and Jennifer Terry. "Transnational Feminist Practices against War." *Meridians: Feminism, Race, Transnationalism* 2, no. 2 (2002): 305.
BBC Mundo. "El 'símbolo' de Panchita," July 7, 2006, accessed September 16, 2019, http://news.bbc.co.uk/hi/spanish/specials/2006/trabajadoras_hogar/newsid_5096000/5096072.stm.

Beaubien, Jason. "Peru Has the World's Highest COVID Death Rate. Here's Why," *NPR's Morning Edition*, November 27, 2021, https://www.npr.org/sections/goatsandsoda/2021/11/27/1057387896/peru-has-the-worlds-highest-covid-death-rate-heres-why.

Blofield, Merike. *Care Work and Class: Domestic Workers' Struggle for Equal Rights in Latin America*. University Park: Penn State University Press, 2012.

Bueno-Hansen, Pascha. *Feminist and Human Rights Struggles in Peru: Decolonizing Transitional Justice*. Chicago: University of Illinois Press, 2015.

Bunster, Ximena, and Elsa M. Chaney. *Sellers and Servants: Working Women in Lima, Peru*. Photography by Ellan Young. New York: Praeger Publishers, 1985.

Burt, Jo-Marie. "Accounting for Murder: The Contested Narratives of the Life and Death of María Elena Moyano." In *Accounting for Violence: Marketing Memory in Latin America*. Edited by Ksenija Bilbija and Leigh A. Payne, 69–95. Durham, NC: Duke University Press, 2011.

———. *Political Violence and the Authoritarian State in Peru: Silencing Civil Society*. New York: Palgrave MacMillan, 2007.

Canal N. "Manuel Burga Díaz fue designado director del LUM," August 6, 2018, https://canaln.pe/actualidad/manuel-burga-diaz-fue-designado-director-lum-n333223.

Carrión, Julio F., ed. *The Fujimori Legacy: The Rise of Electoral Authoritarianism in Peru*. University Park: Penn State University Press, 2006.

Castañeda, Rosmery Anni Barrientos. "Análisis del discurso de la canción 'Flor de Retama' en la formación de la identidad cultural en pobladores Ayacuchanos." Thesis, Universidad de César Vallejo, 2018, https://repositorio.ucv.edu.pe/bitstream/handle/20.500.12692.

Cho, Sumi, Kimberlé Williams Crenshaw, and Leslie McCall. "Toward a Field of Intersectionality Studies: Theory, Applications, and Praxis." *Signs: Journal of Women in Culture and Society* 38, no. 4 (2013): 785–810.

Choo, Hae Yeon, and Myra Marx Ferree. "Practicing Intersectionality in Sociological Research: A Critical Analysis of Inclusions, Interactions, and Institutions in the Study of Inequalities." *Sociological Theory* 28, no. 2 (2010): 129–49.

Colchado, Gladys Pereyra. "Nueva ley de trabajadoras del hogar: estos son los cambios aprobados," September 5, 2020, https://elcomercio.pe/lima/sucesos/trabajadoras-del-hogar-los-15-cambios-en-las-condiciones-laborales-que-se-busca-con-nueva-ley-pleno-mujer-coronavirus-peru-covid-19-cuarentena-noticia/.

Collyns, Dan. "Mayor Closes Museum of Memories in Battle over Story of Peru's Violent Past," *The Guardian*, April 7, 2023, https://www.theguardian.com/world/2023/apr/07/peru-mayor-closes-museum-of-memories-army-shining-path.

Comisión de la Verdad y Reconciliación. "Informe Final," 2003, accessed October 16, 2017, http://www.cverdad.org.pe/ifinal/index.php.

———. Press Release 226, "TRC Final Report was made public on August 28th 2003 at noon," accessed September 1, 2021, https://www.cverdad.org.pe/ingles/pagina01.php.

Degregori, Carlos Iván. *How Difficult It Is to Be God: Shining Path's Politics of War in Peru, 1980–1999*. Madison: University of Wisconsin Press, 2012.

Delfín, Victor. *Delfín: Paintings and Sculptures*. Lima: IMADIS Comunicadores, 2000.

———. "Inside the Artist's Studio: A Visit with Victor Delfín." Goshen.edu, March 25, 2014, accessed October 16, 2017, https://www.goshen.edu/peru/2014/03/25/inside-the-artists-studio-a-visit-with-victor-delfin/.

Dosek, Tomas, and Maritza Parendes, "Peru Might Elect an Authoritarian President: These Four Maps Tell You Why," *Washington Post*, June 3, 2016, https://www.washingtonpost.com/news/monkey-cage/wp/2016/06/03/peru-might-elect-an-authoritarian-president-these-four-maps-tell-you-whos-voting-how-and-why/.

Drinot, Paulo. *The Allure of Labor: Workers, Race, and the Making of the Peruvian State*. Durham, NC: Duke University Press, 2011.

———. "For Whom the Eye Cries: Memory, Monumentality, and the Ontologies of Violence in Peru." *Journal of Latin American Cultural Studies* 18, no. 1 (2009): 23.

El Peruano. "Declaran Patrimonio Cultural de la Nación al memorial 'El Ojo que Llora' de propiedad de la Asociación Civil Caminos de la Memoria," January 21, 2021, https://busquedas.elperuano.pe/dispositivo/NL/2033038-1/.

Encarnación, Omar G. *Democracy Without Justice in Spain: The Politics of Forgetting*. Philadelphia: University of Pennsylvania Press, 2014.

Enloe, Cynthia. *The Curious Feminist: Searching for Women in a New Age of Empire*. Berkeley: University of California Press, 2004.

Estévez, Alejandro M., and Susana C. Esper. "La relación entre el Sistema impositivo y la desigualdad: El papel de la Administración Tributaria en la cohesión social." Working Paper 19, Observatory on Inequality in Latin America, University of Miami, 2019.

Ewig, Christina. "Hijacking Global Feminism: Feminists, the Catholic Church, and the Family Planning Debacle in Peru." *Feminist Studies* 32, no. 3 (2006): 632–59.

Facing History. "Responding to the Insurrection at the U.S. Capitol," January 4, 2022 (updated), https://www.facinghistory.org/educator-resources/current-events/responding-insurrection-us-capitol.

Falcón, Julissa Mantilla. "Gender and Human Rights: Lessons from the Peruvian Truth and Reconciliation Commission." In *Feminist Agendas and Democracy in Latin America*, ed. Jane S. Jaquette, 129–42. Durham, NC: Duke University Press, 2009, https://doi.org/10.1515/9780822392569-008.

Falcón, Sylvanna M. "Intersectionality and the Arts: Counterpublic Memory-Making in Postconflict Peru," *International Journal of Transitional Justice* 12, no. 1 (2018): 26–44.

———. *Power Interrupted: Antiracist Feminist Activism inside the United Nations*. Seattle: University of Washington Press, 2016.

———. "Transnational Feminism and Contextualized Intersectionality at the 2001 World Conference against Racism." *Journal of Women's History* 24, no. 4 (2012): 99–120.

Farell, Emily, and Kathy Seipp. *The Road to Peace: A Teaching Guide on Local and Global Transitional Justice*. Minneapolis: The Advocates for Human Rights, 2008.

Feldman, Joseph P. *Memories before the State: Postwar Peru and the Place of Memory, Tolerance, and Social Inclusion*. New Brunswick, NJ: Rutgers University Press, 2021.

———. "Yuyanapaq No Entra: Ritual Dimensions of Post-Transitional Justice in Peru." *Journal of the Royal Anthropological Institute*, n.s., 24 (2018): 589–606.

Felski, Rita. *Beyond Feminist Aesthetics: Feminist Literature and Social Change*. Boston, MA: Harvard University Press, 1989.

Fernandes, Leela. *Transnational Feminism in the United States: Knowledge, Ethics, Power*. New York: New York University Press, 2013.

Fraser, Nancy. "Rethinking the Public Sphere: A Contribution to the Critique of Actually Existing Democracy." *Social Text* 25, no. 26 (1990): 56–80.

Freire, Paulo. *Pedagogy of the Oppressed*. Translated by Myra Bergman Ramos. New York: Seabury Press, 1970.

———. *Pedagogy of Hope*. New York: Continuum, 1994.

Gómez-Barris, Macarena. *Where Memory Dwells: Culture and State Violence in Chile*. Berkeley: University of California Press, 2009.

Gordon, Avery F. *Ghostly Matters: Haunting and the Sociological Imagination*. Minneapolis: University of Minnesota Press, 2008.

Gutiérrez-Rodríguez, Encarnación. *Migration, Domestic Work, and Affect: A Decolonial Approach on Value and the Feminization of Labor*. New York: Routledge, 2010.

Hancock, Ange-Marie. *Intersectionality: An Intellectual History*. New York: Oxford University Press, 2016.

———. "When Multiplication Doesn't Equal Quick Addition: Examining Intersectionality as a Research Paradigm." *Perspectives on Politics* 5, no. 1 (2007): 63–79.

"Hatun Willakuy: Abbreviated Version of the Peruvian Final Report of the Truth and Reconciliation Commission." The Center for Civil and Human Rights of the University of Notre Dame, the Instituto de Democracia y Derechos Humanos de la Pontificia Universidad Católica del Perú, and the International Center for Transitional Justice, February 2004 (Spanish ed.); August 2010 and May 2014 (English ed.), https://www.ictj.org/sites/default/files/ICTJ_Book_Peru_CVR_2014.pdf.

Heiberg, Marianne, Brendan O'Leary, and John Tirman, eds. *Terror, Insurgency, and the State: Ending Protracted Conflicts*. Philadelphia: University of Pennsylvania Press, 2007.

Heilman, Jaymie. "Truth and Reconciliation Commission of Peru." *Oxford Research Encyclopedia of Latin American History*, June 25, 2018, https://oxfordre.com/latinamericanhistory/view/10.1093/acrefore/9780199366439.001.0001/acrefore-9780199366439-e-495?print=pdf.

Hilgers, Lauren. "Out of the Shadows," *New York Times Magazine*, February 21, 2019, https://www.nytimes.com/interactive/2019/02/21/magazine/national-domestic-workers-alliance.html.

Hite, Katherine. "'The Eye That Cries': The Politics of Representing Victims in Contemporary Peru." *A Contracorriente* 5, no. 1 (2007): 108–34.

———. *Politics and the Art of Commemoration: Memorials to Struggle in Latin America and Spain.* New York: Routledge, 2012.

Human Rights Watch, "Deadly Decline: Security Force Abuses and Democratic Crisis in Peru," April 26, 2023, https://www.hrw.org/report/2023/04/26/deadly-decline/security-force-abuses-and-democratic-crisis-peru#6756.

Jelin, Elizabeth. "The Minefields of Memory." North American Congress on Latin America, September 25, 2007, https://nacla.org/article/minefields-memory.

———. "Silences, Visibility, and Agency: Ethnicity, Class, and Gender in Public Memorialization." In *Identities in Transition: Challenges for Transitional Justice in Divided Societies*, ed. Paige Arthur, 187–213. New York: Cambridge University Press, 2011. (An earlier and abbreviated version appeared in International Center for Transitional Justice research brief, June 2009, accessed October 16, 2017, https://www.ictj.org/sites/default/files/ICTJ-Identities-Memory-ResearchBrief-2009-English.pdf/.)

Johns Hopkins University and Medicine, Coronavirus Resource Center, "Mortality in the most affected countries," March 16, 2023, https://coronavirus.jhu.edu/data/mortality.

Kirk, Robin. *The Monkey's Paw: New Chronicles from Peru.* Amherst: University of Massachusetts Press, 1997.

Klein, Naomi. *Shock Doctrine: The Rise of Disaster Capitalism.* New York: Picador, 2008.

Lang, James M. *Small Teaching: Everyday Lessons from the Science of Learning.* San Francisco, CA: Jossey-Bass, 2016.

La República. "El ojo que llora: Monumento fue atacado nuevamente y familiares exigen mayor seguridad." March 3, 2017, https://larepublica.pe/politica/853467-el-ojo-que-llora-monumento-fue-atacado-nuevamente-y-familiares-exigen-mayor-seguridad.

———. "Solo 34% de peruanos conoce la comisión que investigó violencia terrorista," November 18, 2013, www.larepublica.pe/18-11-2013/solo-34-de-peruanos-conoce-la-comision-que-investigo-violencia-terrorista (last access August 1, 2022).

———. "Yuyachkani presenta: Sin Título técnica mixta—Revisado," May 10, 2018, accessed March 10, 2019, https://larepublica.pe/cultural/1240450-yuyachkani-presenta-titulo-tecnica-mixta-revisado/.

La Serna, Miguel. *Corner of the Living: Ayacucho on the Eve of the Shining Path Insurgency.* Chapel Hill: University of North Carolina Press, 2012.

Lehrer, Erica, and Cynthia E. Milton. "Introduction: Witnesses to Witnessing." In *Curating Difficult Knowledge: Violent Pasts in Public Places*, edited by Erica Lehrer, Cynthia Milton, and Monica Patterson, 1–19. London: Palgrave Macmillan, 2011.

Li, Fabiana. *Unearthing Conflict: Corporate Mining, Activism, and Expertise in Peru*. Durham, NC: Duke University Press, 2015.

Llosa, Mario Vargas. "El ojo que llora." *El Pais*, January 14, 2007, http://elpais.com/diario/2007/01/14/opinion/1168729205_850215.html.

Loehwing, Melanie, and Jeff Motter. "Publics, Counterpublics, and the Promise of Democracy." *Philosophy and Rhetoric* 42, no. 3 (2009): 220–41.

Lugones, Maria C. "Toward a Decolonial Feminism." *Hypatia* 25, no. 4 (2010): 742–59.

Lugones, Maria C., and Elizabeth V. Spelman. "Have We Got a Theory for You! Feminist Theory, Cultural Imperialism, and the Demands for 'The Woman's Voice.'" In *Women's Studies International Forum* 6, no. 6 (1983): 573–81, https://doi.org/10.1016/0277-5395(83)90019-5.

LUM, "Para recordar Yuyanapaq: 15 años después" press release, accessed July 16, 2022, https://lum.cultura.pe/exposiciones/para-recordar-yuyanapaq-15-a%C3%B1os-despu%C3%A9s.

———. "Diálogo Reimaginar el LUM: Los museos de memoria en el Perú," LUM webinar, YouTube, May 29, 2021, https://www.youtube.com/watch?v=4gl9DSYaHXA.

Lust, Jan. "Social Struggle and the Political Economy of Natural Resource Extraction in Peru." *Critical Sociology* 42, no. 2 (March 2016): 200. doi:10.1177/0896920513501354.

Mauceri, Philip. "State Reform, Coalitions, and the Neoliberal Autogolpe." *Latin American Research Review* 30, no. 1 (1995): 8.

Milton, Cynthia E., ed. *Art from a Fractured Past: Memory and Truth Telling in Post-Shining Path Peru*. Durham, NC: Duke University Press, 2014.

———. *Conflicted Memory: Military Cultural Interventions and the Human Rights Era in Peru*. Madison: University of Wisconsin Press, 2018.

———. "Curating Memories of Armed State Actors in Peru's Era of Transitional Justice." *Memory Studies* 8, no. 3 (2015): 361–78.

———. "Defacing Memory: (Un)tying Peru's Memory Knots." In *Curating Difficult Knowledge: Violent Pasts in Public Places*, edited by Erica Lehrer, Cynthia E. Milton, and Monica Patterson, 1–19. London: Palgrave Macmillan, 2011.

Moraga, Cherríe. Interview by Kelly Anderson, video recording, June 6, 2005, Voices of Feminism Oral History Project, Sophia Smith Collection, tape 5, pages 82–83 of transcript, accessed November 10, 2019, https://www.smith.edu/libraries/libs/ssc/vof/transcripts/Moraga.pdf.

Ong, Aihwa. "Powers of Sovereignty: State, People, Wealth, Life." *Focaal—Journal of Global and Historical Anthropology* 64 (2012): 24–35. doi:10.3167/fcl.2012.640103.

Perry, Ellen, producer and director. *The Fall of Fujimori*. Burbank, CA: Cinema Libre Studio/Stardust Pictures, 2006.

Pitarch, Pedro, Shannon Speed, and Xochitl Leyva Solano, eds. *Human Rights in the Maya Region: Global Politics, Moral Engagements, and Cultural Contentions*. Durham, NC: Duke University Press, 2008.

Planas, Enrique. "Lika Mutal murio: Lee nuestra entrevista inédita con la artista." *El Comercio*, November 8, 2016, accessed October 16, 2017, https://elcomercio.pe/luces/arte/lika-mutal-murio-lee-nuestra-entrevista-inedita-artista-noticia-1944982.

Ramírez, Catherine S., Sylvanna M. Falcón, Steve McKay, Juan Poblete, and Felicity Amaya Schaeffer. *Precarity and Belonging: Labor, Migration, and Noncitizenship*. New Brunswick, NJ: Rutgers University Press, 2021.

Rochabrun, Marcelo. "Inter-American Court Orders Peru Not to Release Fujimori from Prison," *Reuters*, April 8, 2022, https://www.reuters.com/world/americas/inter-american-court-orders-peru-not-release-fujimori-prison-2022-04-08/.

Romero, Simon. "As Ex-President Faces Trial, a Reckoning for Peru." *New York Times*, September 25, 2007, accessed January 18, 2020, https://www.nytimes.com/2007/09/25/world/americas/25peru.html.

Root, Rebecca. *Transitional Justice in Peru*. New York: Palgrave MacMillan, 2012.

Salazar, Estevan. "Reglamento de la ley de trabajadoras del hogar entra en vigencia desde hoy," *La Republica*, April 18, 2021, accessed September 14, 2021, https://larepublica.pe/economia/2021/04/18/ley-de-trabajadoras-del-hogar-entra-en-vigencia-desde-hoy/.

Salcedo, Jose Maria. "Con Sendero en Lurigancho." *Quehacer* 39 (1986): 60-67.

Saona, Margarita. *Memory Matters in Transitional Peru*. New York: Palgrave Macmillan, 2014.

Scott, James. *Seeing Like a State: How Certain Schemes to Improve the Human Condition Have Failed*. New Haven, CT: Yale University Press, 1997.

Segato, Rita L. "A Manifesto in Four Themes." Translated by Ramsey McGlazer. *Critical Times* 1, no. 1 (2018): 198–211.

Starn, Orin. "Maoism in the Andes: The Communist Party of Peru-Shining Path and the Refusal of History." *Journal of Latin American Studies* 27, no. 2 (May 1995): 399–421.

Statista. "Level of Education of the Population Aged 25 and Older in Peru in 2017, by Area of Residence," accessed July 12, 2022, https://www.statista.com/statistics/705969/education-level-population-of-peru-area-of-residence/.

Stephenson, Marcia. "Forging an Indigenous Counterpublic Sphere: The Taller de Historia Oral Andina in Bolivia." *Latin American Research Review* 37, no. 2 (2002): 99–118.

Stepputat, Finn, and Ninna Nyberg Sørensen. "IDPs and Mobile Livelihoods." *Forced Migration Review* 14 (July 2002), https://www.fmreview.org/older-displaced-people/stepputat-sorensen.

Strong, Mary. *Art, Nature, and Religion in the Central Andes: Themes and Variations from Prehistory to the Present*. Austin: University of Texas Press, 2012.

Superintendencia Nacional de Fiscalización Laboral, "Nueva Ley de Trabajadoras y Trabajadores del Hogar," https://www.gob.pe/institucion/sunafil/campa%C3%B1as/2866-nueva-ley-de-trabajadoras-y-trabajadores-del-hogar.

Taj, Mitra. "Peru's Top Court Reinstates Pardon for Former President Alberto Fujimori." *New York Times*, March 17, 2022, https://www.nytimes.com/2022/03/17/world/americas/peru-alberto-fujimori.html.

Taylor, Diana. *Disappearing Acts: Spectacles of Gender and Nationalism in Argentina's "Dirty War."* Durham, NC: Duke University Press.

Tegel, Simeon. "Pedro Castillo Finally Declared Winner of Peru's Presidential Election," *Washington Post*, July 19, 2021, https://www.washingtonpost.com/world/2021/07/19/castillo-wins-peru-election/.

Teitel, Ruth G. *Transitional Justice.* New York: Oxford University Press, 2002.

———. "Transitional Justice Genealogy." *Harvard Human Rights Journal* 16 (2003): 69–94.

Theidon, Kimberly. "Disarming the Subject: Remembering War and Imagining Citizenship in Peru." *Cultural Critique* 54 (Spring 2003): 67.

———. *Intimate Enemies: Violence and Reconciliation in Peru.* Philadelphia: University of Pennsylvania Press, 2013.

TV Perú Noticias, "Presidente Dina Boluarte en Piura, hoy martes 14 de junio del 2023," https://www.youtube.com/watch?v=sNdkUUAJg5Y and https://www.tvperu.gob.pe/noticias/politica/dina-boluarte-no-somos-un-gobierno-que-no-mira-sus-errores.

Vich, Victor. *Poéticas de duelo: Ensayos sobre arte, memoria, y violencia política en el Perú.* Lima, Perú: Instituto de Estudios Peruanos, 2015.

Walker, Charles F. *The Tupac Amaru Rebellion.* Cambridge, MA: Harvard University Press, 2016.

Weld, Kirsten. *Paper Cadavers: The Archives of Dictatorship in Guatemala.* Durham, NC: Duke University Press, 2014.

"Yuyanapaq," Art and Reconciliation: Conflict, Culture and Community, accessed July 16, 2022, https://artreconciliation.org/arts-and-reconciliation/case-studies/yuyanapaq/.

Zarate, Andrea, and Nicholas Casey. "Fujimori Is Ordered back to Prison in Peru, Angering Supporters," *New York Times*, October 3, 2018, https://www.nytimes.com/2018/10/03/world/peru-alberto-fujimori.html.

Index

Note: Page numbers in italic refer to illustrations.

active memory, 6, 20
adolescent program (Panchita), 90–92
AGTR (Asociación Grupo de Trabajo Redes), 71, 73
Agüero, José Carlos, 113–16
Alexander, M. Jacqui, 55–56
AMPAEF (Asociación de Mujeres Peruanas Afectadas por las Esterilizaciones Forzadas), 67, 78, 102
Anderson, Bridget, 14
ANFASEP (Asociación Nacional de Familiares de Secuestrados, Detenidos y Desaparecidos del Perú), 102
Anzaldúa, Gloria, 55–56
Apoyo para el Futuro (Support for the Future) (Panchita), 90–92
APRODEH (La Asociación Pro Derechos Humanos): ANFASEP and, 102; Coordinadora Nacional de Derechos Humanos and, 10; Delfín mural, 36–41, *37*, 48–49; Mutal's El Ojo Que Llora memorial, 41–50, *42*, *43*
Argumedo, Juan, 28
arrepentimiento (repentance), 95–96
art, counterpublic: Delfín's APRODEH mural, 36–41, *37*, 48–49; Delgado's "Un Dia Como Hoy," 67, *68*; intersectionality and, 34–36; memory making through, 25–26, 36; Mutal's El Ojo Que Llora memorial, 41–50, *42*, *43*, 54–56, 103–4, 115; Tarata memorial, 31, *32*, 103; transformative memory and, 49–50; transformative memory flowchart, *107*; *Yuyanapaq* photo exhibition, 18, 23–25, 100–101
Asociación de Mujeres Peruanas Afectadas por las Esterilizaciones Forzadas (AMPAEF), 67, 78, 102
Asociación Grupo de Trabajo Redes (AGTR), 71, 73
Asociación Nacional de Familiares de Secuestrados, Detenidos y Desaparecidos del Perú (ANFASEP), 102
Asociación Pro Derechos Humanos. *See* APRODEH
Aucatoma, Simeón, 28, 121n15
authoritarianism: colonialism and, 76; counterpublics and, 106; COVID-19 pandemic and, 117; of Fujimori, 44, 80; liberalism and, 5; Memory Game and, 59; public support for, 59, 94; transnational, 111. *See also* Fujimori, Alberto
Ayacucho: ANFASEP and, 102; *arrepentimiento* (repentance) practice in, 95; ballot box burning and declaration of war against state, 5, 27; ceremony marking end of CVR work, 20, 99; domestic workers from, 91;

Ayacucho (*continued*): journalists killed in, 28; Pampachacra, 64–65; victim-perpetrator binary and, 100
Ayacucho University, 28

Barrientos Castañeda, Rosmery Anni, 61–62
Barrios Altos massacre, 45
Belaúnde Terry, Fernando, 27
Beso, El (Delfín), 38
Blofield, Merike, 75, 124n19
Bueno-Hansen, Pascha, 10
Burga, Manuel, 100

capitalism: citizenship hierarchy and, 11; as civilizing project, 24; counterpublics and, 12, 36; decolonial feminist analysis and, 5; domestic workers and, 72; Fujimori and, 33; liberalism and, 5, 111; Museo Itinerante Arte por la Memoria and, 25; racist, anti-Indigenous, 14, 71–72
Casa de Panchita, La: about, 1–2, 72–73; Apoyo para el Futuro (Support for the Future) adolescent program, 90–92; childcare workshops, 81–84; as counterpublic, 75, 92–93; elder care workshops, 85–86; environment and home emergencies workshops, 86–87; girls' tutorial program, 17; law workshops, 17, 79–81, 87–90; power dynamics and, 93, 115; transformative memory flowchart, *107*
Castillo, Pedro, 12, 94, 107, 108–9
Ccasani, Manuel, 28, 121n15
Chávez, Martha, 101
citizenship: "failed," "good," and "tolerated" citizens, 14–15; race and, 14, 77
citizenship, tiered: capitalism, white supremacy, and, 11; domestic workers and, 72, 74–75, 92–93; emotion and tears, deep connection to, 3; Fujimori savior narrative and, 106; media coverage and, 105; Memory Game and, 62; scalar model of citizenship, 13
civilizing mission, 78

colonialism, Spanish: domestic workers and, 75, 76; extractive capitalism and, 5; heart weakened by, 96; Memory Game and, 62; multigenerational trauma and, 7
Comisión de la Verdad y Reconciliación (CVR): about, 99; Amnesty International report, 8; citizen categories and, 14–15; media coverage and public debate, 99–102; on military, 113; report, 9, 13, 16, 20, 25, 44, 96, 98–101; unawareness of, 13; *Yuyanapaq* photo exhibit, 18, 23–25
commemoration events, 54–56
community education. *See* education
complex personhood, 76, 80
Condon, Christopher B., 38
Coordinadora Nacional de Derechos Humanos, 10, 102
counterpublics: as critical oppositional forces, 36; defined, 6, 12–13; human rights memory and, 8; Panchita as, 75, 92–93; purpose of, 102–5; reconciliation and, 96–97. *See also* art, counterpublic
coups. *See* self-coups
COVID-19 pandemic, 108, 116–17
CVR. *See* Comisión de la Verdad y Reconciliación

decolonial feminism. *See* feminism and decolonial feminist analysis
Degregori, Carlos Iván, 6, 13
Delfín, Victor, 26, 36–41, 48–49, 51
Delgado, Mauricio, 67, *68*
despazados (the internally displaced), 74, 93
"Dia Como Hoy, Un" (Delgado), 67, *68*
"Diálogo Reimaginar el LUM," 112–13
displacement, internal, 74, 93
Dolorier Urbano, Ricardo, 61–62
domestic workers: complex personhood, hauntings, and, 75–79; contracts, 88–90; displacement and, 74, 93; generational trauma and specters of violence, 82–84, 89, 91–92; hours worked, 79, 124n19; power dynamic, 93; race and, 74; rights of,

79–80, 87–90; *servicio completo* (full service), 84; tiered citizenship and, 72, 74–75, 92–93. See also Casa de Panchita, La
Domestic Workers Law (Ley de las trabajadoras y trabajadores del hogar), 73, 79–81, 85, 88–90, 106
dominant publics. *See* publics, dominant
Drinot, Paul, 11, 14–15, 24, 47, 76–77

education: Ayacucho uprising, 61–62; community-based, on holistic human rights, 57; Memory Game, 56–63; pedagogical triangle, 53–54, 101; right-wing push-back on curriculum, 104; transformative memory flowchart, *107*
Encarnación, Omar G., 97–98
Enloe, Cynthia, 16

Facing History, 53, 63
failed citizens, 14–15
feminism and decolonial feminist analysis: category of citizen, 13–14; change and, 3; counterpublic art and, 41; heart and, 96; human rights memory and, 8; intersectionality and, 47; liberalism and, 5; Memory Game and, 60, 62; praxis, 111; Senderista-person-institution distinction and, 114; spirituality and, 56; transitional justice and, 9–10, 15
Fernandes, Leela, 55–56
Flora Tristan, 18
"Flor de Retama" (Dolorier), 61–62
forgetting (*olvido*), 97–98, 105
forgiveness, 98
Fuerza Popular, 59
Fujimori, Alberto: conviction, sentence, and pardon, 5–6, 95, 106–7, 110; domestic workers' rights and, 74, 80; dominant savior narrative, 105–6; election and reelection of, 27, 33; salvation memory and, 7; scandals, exile, and resignation, 34; second term and state restructuring, 33–34; self-coup (1992), 26, 31–33; sterilization campaign, 67, 78; trial of, 4, 38

Fujimori, Keiko, 6, 12, 38, 59, 94, 107, 109–10

García, Alan, 9, 27, 32–33, 110
García, Amador, 28
Gavilán, Félix, 28
gendered violence. *See* violence, gender-based and sexual
generational trauma, 7–8, 76, 82–84, 96
ghosts and hauntings, 75–79, 102–6
Gonzalo Thought, 29
Gordon, Avery F., 75–76, 78, 103
Grupo Colina, 30–31
guilt, 113–14
Gutiérrez Rodríguez, Encarnación, 78–79
Guzmán, Abimael, 27–28, 29, 33

hauntings and ghosts, 75–79, 102–6
heart, 95–96, 105–6, 115
Hite, Katherine, 41, 44–45, 47
Huaychao, 27
human-centric vs. Indigenous cosmologies, 12
human rights counterpublics. *See* art, counterpublic; counterpublics
human rights culture: art and, 69–70; counterpublics and, 13; cultivating, 92–93; legal protections and, 90; Panchita and, 72
human rights memory: activating, 98, 105, 106, *107*, 110; Agüero on, 114–15; counterpublic art and backlash, 25, 36, 41, 49; decolonial feminism and, 3–13; deserving vs. undeserving victims and, 48–49; Memory Game and, 57–60; Museo Itinerante and, 69; as narrative, 7–8; politicized, 112–17; salvation memory vs., 7–8

Indigenous communities: Boluarte's anti-Indigenous discourse, 109; "de-Indianization of Peru," 14, 15, 24, 77; racist, anti-Indigenous capitalism, 14, 71–72. *See also* racism
industrialization, haunting of, 76–77
Infante, Octavio, 28

Inicio de la Lucha Armada, 27–28
Inter-American Court of Human Rights (IACHR), 44, 46–47, 107
internal conflict, Peruvian (1980–2000): about, 1; Barrios Altos massacre, 45; *despazados* (the internally displaced), 74, 93; first time period (1980–1992), 26–31; human rights organizations during, 10–11; *Inicio de la Lucha Armada*, 27–28; Lucanamarca massacre, 27–28; second time period (1992–2000), 31–34; transitional justice and, 2. *See also* Comisión de la Verdad y Reconciliación; Fujimori, Alberto; Sendero Luminoso
intersectionality: counterpublic art and, 34–36; defined, 35; domestic workers and, 75; feminist theory, 47

Jelin, Elizabeth, 26, 35, 47, 97, 98, 110
Jiménez, Edilberto, 62
justice, transitional. *See* transitional justice

Kirk, Robin, 121n15
Kuczynski, Pedro Pablo (PPK), 6, 106

Lazzara, Michael, 113–14
Ledgard, Denise, 19, 100
Lehrer, Erica, 25–26
León, Enrique, 112–13
Lerner, Salomón, 19, 20, 95
Li, Fabiana, 11
liberalism: authoritarianism and, 111; capitalism and, 5, 111; decolonial feminist analysis and, 5; multigenerational trauma and, 7
López Aliaga, Rafael, 116
Lucanamarca massacre, 27–28
Lugar de la Memoria, la Tolerancia y la Inclusión Social (LUM), 18–19, 99–101, 112–13, 115–16
Lugar de la Memoria (Place of Memory) project, 63
Lugones, Maria, 55–56

Marxism, Peruvian-style, 29–30
Mauceri, Philip, 31–32

media coverage, 99–102
memorials: El Ojo Que Llora (Mutal), 41–50, *42*, *43*, 54–56, 103–4; Tarata, 31, *32*, 103
memory: active, 6, 20; conflicted, 53; minefields of, 112; postmemory generation, 23–25, 51–52, 96, 104, 115; salvation memory narrative, 7–8, 18; thread of, 111–12; "too much," 96; universal memory narrative vs. memory recovery, 113. *See also* human rights memory; transformative memory
memory making: artistic, 52; intersectionality and, 35; Memory Game and, 59–60; military and, 113; through art, 25–26, 36
memory recovery through art and education: about, 52–53; Memory Clock Game (El Reloj de Memoria), 56–63; Museo Itinerante Arte por la Memoria, 63–69; El Ojo Que Llora commemoration event, 54–56; pedagogical triangle and, 53–54; *Sin Título* (Yuyachkani), 51–52; transformative memory flowchart, *107*
Mendivil, Jorge Luis, 28
Mendoza, Verónika, 110
Miguel Castro Castro Prison raid, 44
military and memory production, 113
Milton, Cynthia, 7, 25–26, 48, 53, 113
Montesinos, Vladimiro, 34
Moraga, Cherríe, 83
Morales, Dionisio, 28, 121n15
Movimiento Revolucionario de Túpac Amaru (MRTA), 7, 11, 34, 121n31
Moyano, María Elena, 18, 30, *30*, 63, 123n18
MRTA (Movimiento Revolucionario de Túpac Amaru), 7, 11, 34, 121n31
Museo Itinerante Arte por la Memoria, 63–69, 102
Museo Nacional, 18, 23–25, 100–101
Mutal, Lika, 41–46, 50

national identity, new, 104
Navarez, Rosario "Charro," 36, 39, 46, 55
newspaper coverage, 99–102

Ojo Que Llora, El (Mutal), 41–50, *42, 43*, 54–56, 103–4, 115
olvido (forgetting), 97–98, 105

Pachamama (Mother Earth), 43–45, 56, 103
Pampachacra, 64–65
Panchita. *See* Casa de Panchita, La
Paniagua, Valentín, 34
patriarchy: decolonial feminism and, 5, 8; Delfín mural and, 39; forced sterilization campaign and, 67; haunting and, 104; intersectionality and, 36; labor, feminization of, 78–79; Peruvian state built on, 14; Segato on fantasy that sustains, 111
pedagogical triangle, 53–54, 101
personhood, complex, 76, 80
Peruvian internal conflict. *See* internal conflict, Peruvian
Piniella, Eduardo de la, 28
positive forgetfulness, 98
postmemory generation, 23–25, 51–52, 96, 104, 115
PPK (Pedro Pablo Kuczynski), 6
protests: Boluarte and, 108–10; Fujimori pardon, 106–7; Huanta, 61–62; mining conflicts, 11–12
publics, dominant: art backlash by, 25, 34–36, 40–41; Boluarte and anti-Indigenous discourse, 109; counternarrative in art and education, 69; defined, 12; difficult knowledge and, 26; Fujimorismo and, 22, 105–6; Peruvian state formation, counterpublics, and, 12–15; salvation memory and, 8; transitional justice and, 9, 19; "victim," constructions of, 48–49

Quipu Project, 15

racism: anti-Indigenous capitalism, 14, 71–72; Boluarte's anti-Indigenous discourse, 109; capitalism, racist and anti-Indigenous, 14, 71–72; citizenship and, 14, 77; "de-Indianization of Peru," 14, 15, 24, 77; domestic workers and, 74; Museo Itinerante Arte por la Memoria and, 25; Peruvian state built on, 14
rape. *See* violence, gender-based and sexual
reconciliation, 96–97, 100
Reloj de Memoria, El (The Memory Clock) game, 56–63
reparations, 104
repentance (*arrepentimiento*), 95–96
Repentance Law (1992), 33
Retto, Willy, 28
rondas campesinas (peasant counterinsurgency militias), 27
Root, Rebecca, 11, 95

salvation memory narrative, 7–8, 18
Sánchez-Gavidia, Pedro, 28
San Juan de Miraflores, 17
Saona, Margarita, 47
Sedano, Jorge, 28
Segato, Rita, 111–12
self-coups: Castillo (2022, failed), 108–9; Fujimori (1992), 26, 31–33
Senderistas: about, 27–29; *arrepentimiento* (repentance) and, 95; Moyano assassination, 30, 63; El Ojo Que Llora monument and, 44, 46, 48–49; Senderista-person-institution distinction, 114
Sendero Luminoso (Shining Path): about, 2; human rights memory and, 7; human rights organizations and, 11; Moyano assassination and Tarata bombing, 30–31; rise of, in Ayacucho, 27–28; Senderista-person-institution distinction, 114; *Yuyanapaq* exhibit and, 18. *See also* internal conflict, Peruvian
sexual violence. *See* violence, gender-based and sexual
Shining Path. *See* Sendero Luminoso
Sin Título (Yuyachkani), 19, 51–52
Sørensen, Ninna Nyberg, 74
Spain, 97–98
spirituality, 55–56
Starn, Orin, 28–29
Stepputat, Finn, 74
sterilization campaign, forced, 67, *68*, 78

Index   139

symbolic progress, 95

Tarata bombing and memorial, Miraflores, 31, *32*, 103
Taylor, Diana, 103–5
Theidon, Kimberly, 95–96, 98
"The Roots of War and Peace" (Advocates for Human Rights, Minneapolis), 9–10
tiers of citizenship. *See* citizenship, tiered
Toledo, Alejandro, 9, 20
transformative memory: counterpublic art and, 41, 49–50; counterpublics and, 13; decolonial praxis, 111; "Diálogo Reimaginar el LUM" and, 113; Memory Game and, 59–60; nonlinear, 94, 106, *107*; Panchita and, 72; public debate and, 99–100; today, 110
transitional justice: about, 3–4; active memory and, 6; decolonial feminism and, 9–10, 15; domestic workers and, 74–75; juridical and political, 6–9; national context and, 98; as nonlinear, 94; official end of internal conflict and, 2
trauma, multigenerational, 7–8, 76, 82–84, 96
tree metaphor, 9–10
Trump, Donald, 110

trust, 97

Vargas Llosa, Mario, 54, 123n7
Velasco Alvarado, Juan, 61–62
victim classification and victim-perpetrator binary, 44, 46–48, 100, 103, 114
Villa El Salvador, 63
violence, gender-based and sexual: CVR and, 15; domestic workers and, 83–84, 89, 91–92
violence, social: defined, 3; hauntings, 75–76, 78, 104; human rights counterpublics and, 96–97; roots of, 4

Walker, Charles, 113–14
white supremacy: citizenship hierarchy and, 11; decolonial feminism and, 5; domestic workers and, 72; liberalism and, 111
women: in Delfín mural, 39; emergent future and, 111; forced sterilization campaign, 67, *68*, 78. *See also* Casa de Panchita, La; domestic workers

Yuyachkani, 19, 51–52
Yuyanapaq photo exhibit (Museo Nacional), 18, 23–25, 100–101

Zavala, Pablo, 56–57

SYLVANNA M. FALCÓN is a professor in Latin American and Latino/a Studies at the University of California Santa Cruz. She is the author of *Power Interrupted: Antiracist and Feminist Activism inside the United Nations* and coeditor of *Precarity and Belonging: Labor, Migration, and Noncitizenship*.

The University of Illinois Press
is a founding member of the
Association of University Presses.
_____

University of Illinois Press
1325 South Oak Street
Champaign, IL 61820-6903
www.press.uillinois.edu